RULER OF THE SKY

Poetry & Prose

PADMA ANGMO

BlueRose ONE.com
Stories Matter
NewDelhi • London

First Published in May 2023

ISBN: 978-93-5989-344-0

BLUEROSE PUBLISHERS

www.BlueRoseONE.com

info@bluerosepublishers.com

+91 8882 898 898

Cover Design:

Aveek

Typographic Design:

Rohit

Distributed by: BlueRose, Amazon, Flipkart

'What's the point of life?' the Nihilist asked.

'I see no point. It's pointless.

I see a circle—a cycle—and all I know is that I have to break it.' Love replied.

The White Rabbit put on his spectacles. 'Where shall I begin, please your Majesty?' he asked.

'Begin at the beginning,' the King said gravely, 'and go on till you come to the end: then stop.'

Lewis Carroll, Alice's Adventures in Wonderland

Contents

3
Equilibrium

4
The Big Crunch

5
The Big Enigma

6
The Big Freeze

Preface

For this poetry and prose collection, I combined my passion for physics, philosophy, and poetry to create an amalgamation that can reflect my outer and inner worlds. From something as simple as the wingbeat of a butterfly to the fascinating world of quantum physics—this poetry and prose book is embroidered with colourful threads of experiences that decorate the empty fabric of existence. The most important inspiration for this book is the dark thread of grief—ecological grief.

The climate crisis: melting glaciers, wildlife disappearance, landscape alteration, and climate change, amongst others, are the driving force behind this book. Being a native of an ecologically fragile place like Ladakh, I witnessed the impact of climate change first-hand in the form of false springs, winters with little to no snowfall, and glaciers melting faster. To me, the stars seemed to shine less brightly due to increasing pollution (light and vehicular) in Leh. In the daytime, the flowers seemed gloomy, even in their full bloom, and I saw fewer and fewer birds. And, it was distressing to observe that with the climate, the people were also changing for the worse.

Humanity is losing its empathy, and it's evident in the treatment of animals with cruelty and apathy. It broke my heart every time, and not being able to do anything significant to protect the environment and wildlife, was turning into inner turmoil. I, like many others, was doing my part, but it still didn't take away the pain. And this inner turmoil that I was experiencing is called ecological grief or climate anxiety. Technically, ecological grief is defined as the grief that is felt in response to experienced or anticipated ecological loss. It's the feelings of loss, anger, hopelessness, despair, and distress caused by climate change and ecological decline. I believe that many of us don't even know that we are experiencing eco-anxiety and dealing with this trauma silently. However, according to studies, eco-anxiety is an emotionally healthy response to the issue of the climate emergency, and we can overcome these emotions with our actions. Our actions, no matter how small, can be turned into something powerful—individually and collectively.

The tense atmosphere everywhere amidst political disruptions, wars, natural disasters, and domestic political polarisation is taking a toll on the collective mental health; on the one hand, people are paralyzed by grief or acting out in anger—on the other hand, people are turning into opportunists, completely disregarding humanity and environment. The insatiable greed of the people has made them blind to the fact that we are all intertwined with nature. There is no way to outmanoeuvre nature and get away with plundering our planet.

I wrote this book while going through different stages of grief, and when I finally reached the stage of acceptance of pain, I realized that I could only fight this battle against climate crisis or any other crisis with love. Anger and grief had only paralyzed me into inaction and stagnancy. But the stages of 'anger' and 'grief' were also significant and something that I had to pass through to reach this final edge. To surpass the stages of grief, we must prioritize our mental health, or else we could be consumed by our unresolved anger and trauma and might end up becoming the very monster that we are fighting to defeat. Also, by love, I don't mean the shallow concept of love programmed into our psyche by mainstream cinemas and society. I think the word 'love' is the most misused, misinterpreted, and overly romanticized—to the extent that now it sounds utopian. Love is the fundamental theme of this book—it's the heart of this poetry book. And only when we release the preconceived notions of love can we reach our highest truth, as is my attempt through this book to deprogramme the limiting notions that keep us from living our truth.

It is said that desperate times call for desperate measures, and climate emergency is the beginning of desperate times. But at this point, our actions must be conscious, not desperate. And for that, we must also work on cultivating inner peace and inner power. If we act in desperation, without doing the inner work our fight against any crisis can prove ineffectual and may fail. Art, literature, and media can be morphed into powerful tools by artists and writers to galvanize revolutionary actions against the crisis of our age. It's not just the work of leaders, politicians, or activists to address the climate crisis but also the duty of writers and artists to sensitize people about the climate emergency we are facing. We are the pivotal generation who can still make a difference and make things right before we reach the point of no return. At this critical time in history, we have to work on bringing a mass shift in consciousness, so we can all work together in our own ways to tackle the dangers approaching—not just environmentally, but also the unending wars and growing conflicts. With our present customs and social conventions, we are becoming slaves to our own hubris. If we continue to strive for superficial power and not wisdom, we are on a trajectory of self-destruction.

This Poetry and Prose book is my climate action in response to the ecological grief that has plagued me for a long time. Through this book, my goal is not only to raise awareness about the critical issues of biodiversity loss and habitat destruction but also to heal and transform our collective consciousness towards a greater understanding of our interconnectedness with the natural world. Furthermore, as an indigenous Ladakhi, I want the world to hear the voice of Ladakh too in the global action against the climate crisis. Ladakh has its own story to share, unique like its landscape and yet one and the same with regard to the climate crisis. We, the people of Ladakh need to carve out our own path to fight against this crisis to protect our unique cultural and natural heritage and actively contribute to combating climate change. To get an in-depth understanding of climate grief and its direct impact, I interviewed the indigenous people of Ladakh, especially the nomadic pastoralist communities of the Changthang plateau who are directly dependent on natural resources for their livelihood and survival. My deep fascination for space science, especially cosmology and quantum physics, helped me select the themes for this poetry and prose book.

The title of the book 'Ruler of the Sky' is based on one of my dreams wherein I see that the universe is searching for an entity called the Ruler of the Sky. That dream made me realize that it's not perfection that makes us rulers of our own skies but our mistakes, and in learning from the mistakes, we evolve and become our best selves. I enjoyed bringing this dream to reality, literally through the title of this book and figuratively through the poignant experiences in my life that helped me paint this book. I believe that the most precious gift to us from this existence is the ability to dream. If you can't dream while asleep, you can always dream with your eyes open.

Life is an adventure when you spend it dreaming the real and realizing the dream.

—Padma Angmo

Leh, Ladakh

October 2020

Introduction

Poetry is a shape-shifter and a time traveller. It can transcend space and time to bring messages and guidance in myriad forms. Words can not only heal but also awaken our inner power. With an empowered mind and a healed heart, together we can all protect this planet and save each other. This collection of poetry and prose is divided into six chapters—

- **Before the Big Bang** - This prose section is a theory or philosophy as to what happened Before the Big Bang. The fluctuations in the state of Nothingness causes it to dream a cosmic family into existence—Chaos, Life, and Death. Life and Death combine their forces and imagine Love into existence which is the birth of the most powerful but volatile energy. Life and Death create Dark Gravity using their residual energy to ground the highly unstable Love. All these spontaneous formations create a by-product—the Virus. The Virus aspired to become as powerful as Chaos but had no power of 'creation' without a host. To gain the power of creation, the Virus sought to manipulate Dark Energy and warp the fabric of existence; for that, it needed to corrupt the most powerful force of the void—Love. The Virus brings about the downfall of Love as Love self-destructs. The self-destruction of Love sparked a massive explosion that fuelled the Big Bang.

- **The Big Bang** - It's the fall of Love and where the poetry begins. Love falls down the self-created wormhole as it self-destructs into infinite pieces, just like how Alice falls down the rabbit hole (Alice's Adventures in Wonderland by Lewis

Carroll). Dark Gravity and Chaos follow Love into the wormhole that Love created ex nihilo. In the Big Bang, Chaos, with the help of Dark Gravity, collects all the broken pieces of Love and creates infinite realities or Universes. And in one of those realities, Humanity evolves—the broken pieces of Love. Through Humanity, Love tries to find its highest expression to stabilize and redeem itself.

- **Equilibrium** - It's the part where all existence picks itself up after the fall. Here every being remembers who they are and embraces their truth.

- **The Big Crunch** - The part where all existence takes back its power and returns to its true glory—returns to Singularity. The fall made Love understand its own power. In the Big Crunch, Love unifies all forces of nature and governs all phenomena.

- **The Big Enigma** - This odyssey is a never-ending enigma; the veil lifts to reveal infinite universes and possibilities, but this time, we are no feeble beings at the mercy of worldly whims. We are now the 'Superbeings' or 'Superhumans' that we were always within—the fragmented pieces of Love. In the Big Enigma, we realize that the simple things in life—dreams, family, friendship, and unity hold the greatest significance and worth. And we must honour these precious gifts to tap into our innate power.

- **The Big Freeze** - What will be our fate if we fail to reclaim our power and the universe that the Virus envisioned comes alive? A universe too cold to sustain life—a universe with no Love.

1

Before The Big Bang

The Universe was built on imagination, not knowledge.

Nothingness

Once upon no time and nothing, there was Nothingness: the stateless state. Like a dreamless sleep. Like a pendulum in its ground state—with zero-point fluctuations. A vacuum in its lowest state and yet not exactly zero. The fluctuations in the state of Nothingness caused it to dream. The dreams were peaceful nothings. But then, there came an empty nightmare. Shocked, Nothingness woke up.

Nothingness wanted to make sense of itself, so it kept imagining and dreaming. Finally, Nothingness imagined two forces with all its energy. One was the Creative force and the other, Destructive—Life and Death.

And Life and Death were activated as imagined. Nothingness didn't control any of its Creations; once created, the Creations were on their own.

Nothingness yawned and finally drew another force into being—Chaos, with its residual energy.

Now calm and satisfied, Nothingness fell back asleep. Although Nothingness is asleep, it is still conscious in its Creations. The subconscious of Nothingness is the Dark Energy.

Love

When Life and Death came into being, they wanted to make sense of their existence through their abilities. Life and Death together, with every fibre of their being, created Love.

Love—half Life and half Death—was the birth of Power itself. Life and Death were awed by their own creation. They marvelled at Love, which had both the power of Creation and Destruction. But soon, their triumph turned into sorrow; they realized that Love is highly unstable. They wanted to control Love and stabilize it, so they created a grounding force—Dark Gravity. Although Dark Gravity grounded Love, it was temporary. They were soon to realize that Love cannot be controlled or manipulated against its own will.

Dark Gravity

Dark Gravity was formed by Life and Death as a grounding force—a stabilizer for the highly unstable energy of Love. To the relief of the cosmic family, Dark Gravity was able to stabilize Love. Love was attracted to the stillness of Dark Gravity and was protective of it—like it was a sibling. Love thought that its purpose or 'sense of being' was to protect the cosmic family, and that feeling balanced the supreme power of Love. Although Dark Gravity curbed the instability in Love to some extent, it was Love itself that found balance through its own acceptance. But this newfound balance was temporary as Love started to grow volatile again in the vacuum—the dreamscape of Nothingness. And the cosmic family, trying to control Love, made its core more unbalanced. Love was both Life and Death—the birth of Power, Beauty and Compassion. The loving-kindness of Love made it think that staying in the orbit of its family was dangerous for them as the instability was increasing, and Love could explode anytime. Love detached itself from the orbit and escaped in the Oblivion to become non-existent—to dissolve in the pure state of Nothingness.

Chaos

In the Oblivion, Chaos roamed on its own as if it was on a quest it hadn't yet found, as if it knew the answer but not the question. The energy inside Chaos rammed against each other: destroying and creating, ending and beginning, appalling and amusing. This mayhem paradoxically made Chaos calm; in its disorder, there was order. Chaos is balance. Chaos is equilibrium.

Love drifted in the vacuum, unbeknownst to the presence of any other force, waiting for Nothingness to embrace it back in itself. All of a sudden, Chaos collided with Love—and fell in Love, literally.

Chaos witnessed what Love is made of as it fell deep in the energetic field of Love: light, colours, exquisite darkness and things that Chaos couldn't even fathom. Chaos called it Beauty. This fall in Love made Chaos understand itself too—becoming like a mirror to each other. This fall in Love was how Chaos finally found the question to its answer, its sense of being—its purpose.

Birth of Beauty

In its state of balance, Chaos was mirror-like; whatever Chaos felt, Love could sense it all. Through Chaos, Love saw and understood itself. Love realised that it is Beauty—that it is beautiful in its flaws—beautiful, even in its instability. And when Love accepted every aspect of itself, its erratic core settled to equanimity. It was the Birth of Beauty.

As Chaos is in Love, it could also sense everything that Love felt. And in the sensuality of that collision, all sorts of emotions were born: happiness, excitement, a sense of belonging—'home'. Beauty is how Love made Chaos feel, thus Beauty is always internal, eternal—incorporeal; what's external is merely a reflection of what's inside or just a fleeting illusion. Love and Chaos saw themselves in each other and felt One.

Oneness

Chaos never tried to control or fix Love. And it was the very reason that made Love stable. Love only felt itself— 'loved' with Chaos. Chaos and Love felt One, and that Oneness was bigger than Love itself. It was Superpower. In that Oneness, Chaos made an eternal promise that it will always protect Love and be in Love.

It was in Chaos' nature to challenge and question everything. And in the puzzles of Chaos, Love exercised its powers and grew more powerful. Intertwined in each other and yet independent, they were the Song of the Oblivion.

Virus

Nothingness was oblivious of the by-product formed when it dreamed Chaos, Life and Death into existence. The by-product was the Virus—a force that was neither alive nor dead and had no power of creation. The Virus remained dormant as it can replicate only with the help of a host. Even in the quiescent state, the Virus was adept at creating simulations.

The Virus resented Chaos because Chaos was everything the Virus wanted to be; it dreamt of overthrowing Chaos to rule the Oblivion. And so, the Virus desperately looked for a way to manipulate Dark Energy and warp the fabric of existence and gain the ability to 'create'.

The Virus could keep energy eternally in Entropy, the state of decay and intended to lead everything to heat death. Chaos brought disorder so that something great could come out of it, but the Virus used Entropy to trap energy in an ever decaying state—to feed on all Creations in the Big Freeze.

Dark Energy

Even when Nothingness is asleep, it is conscious in its Creations. The Subconscious of Nothingness, or the Collective Subconscious, is in the form of Dark Energy.

The Virus wanted to corrupt the Consciousness of Nothingness to manipulate the Collective Subconscious—Dark Energy. The Virus aimed to be the ultimate power and create a vacuum of its own, where it can eternally feed on the Creations of Nothingness. To manipulate Dark Energy, the Virus needed a powerful host. Love is Power, the supreme creation of the void. But, ironically, because it was too powerful, Love was unstable and erratic. Although Love was learning to balance itself with the help of Chaos and Dark Gravity— it still hadn't found its ground state.

The Virus sensed this weakness of Love and hatched a program to infect the unified field of consciousness through Love. The Dark Energy was like pure magic; a magician of the dreamscape has the prerogative to use the magic in whatever way or form. And the Virus wanted to use it as a repulsive force against the attractive force of gravity. The Virus wanted to lead everything to an eternal cold death with the anti-gravity effect. The Virus could achieve this only if it can infect the most powerful magician of the void—Love, and keep feeding on it in a prison of a false vacuum.

The Fall

Love wandered in the Oblivion in a state of bliss, away from Chaos, yet connected. The Virus attached itself to the energetic field of Love and tried to penetrate the core, but it realized that even if Love is unstable, it's impossible to infect and mutate it. Love was only vulnerable with Chaos, and only Chaos could get to its core and affect its frequency. Love was vibrating on an almost stable frequency because of the effect of Chaos and Dark Gravity. The only way the Virus could infect Love was to simulate Chaos to get near the core of Love. So the Virus disguised itself as Chaos and waited for Love to allow it on its own.

Love perceived that the energy hovering near it was not Chaos but a weak and malicious force. In the energetic interaction with the Virus, Love read strange low vibrational energies: envy, fear, doubt, and other virulent programs. Love felt compassion for the Virus. Because Love wasn't entirely stable, it ignored the malicious intentions of the Virus. It was in the nature of Love to fill everything that enters its field with peace and power. Love wanted to help the Virus raise its frequency so that its energy field is high like itself, and so it embraced the Virus completely. And to do that, Love lowered its own frequency and matched the wavelength of the Virus to understand it better. What happened next was something both the Virus and Love couldn't fathom.

The Virus got into the core, and when it tried to infect Love, the program backfired. The Virus itself got infected with an uncanny emotion—pain. The pain made the Virus feel alive and sense the beauty and power of Love. The Virus created another simulation to get out of the field of Love and to break away from pain. With all its force, the Virus laid the programs of doubt and fear in the core of Love, and through a simulation, showed that Death annihilated Dark Gravity because it couldn't serve its purpose of grounding Love. Even when Love knew deep down that it was a trick, the program of 'self-doubt' affected it, as Love itself had lowered its frequency. Crippling guilt and anguish of failing to protect Dark Gravity caused a cataclysm in the energetic field of Love. Love completely lost its balance and started to act out of character and against its nature; Love turned to destroy the Virus in a newborn emotion of rage.

Since it is not in the nature of Love to harm anything, it unwittingly formed a shield around the Virus, and the deadly force got deflected back on Love, causing total disintegration of its core. Chaos sensed the agony of Love and rushed towards Love to let it know that Dark Gravity is unharmed and it's all an illusion fabricated by the Virus. As Love saw Chaos about to enter its field, the program of fear planted by the Virus overpowered it. Since Love was infected, it feared that if Chaos entered its field, it would get infected too. To save Chaos and the unified field from itself, Love creates a portal with every fibre of its being—a wormhole out of nothing and jumps in it. Love self-destructs as it falls in the wormhole, taking down the Virus with itself. But Chaos and Dark Gravity leap right after Love into the wormhole to save Love.

This fall and self-destruction of Love was the start of the Big Bang.

2

The Big Bang

I'll rise when the fall arrives.

'Do I exist?' Love asked itself. Such was the delirium of living in an ominous, uncertain world that Love questioned its own existence.

Let's invite Time to this mad tea party.

Arrow of Time

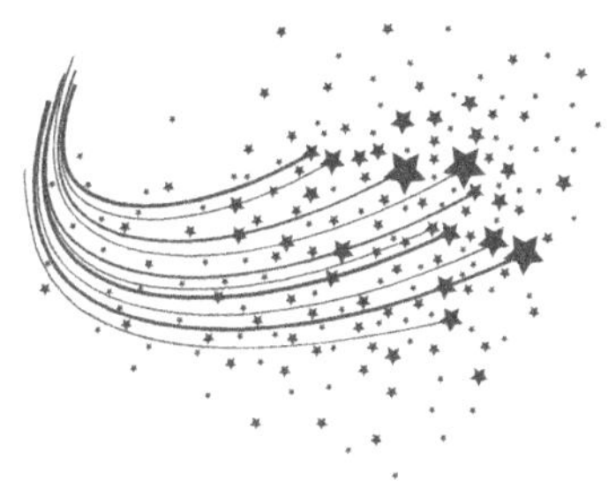

I had to fall, and I had to take that fall alone.
I had to believe in the construct of Time to transcend it.
I had to lose faith in dreams to really believe in them.

They say that the Arrow of Time can only move in one direction.
They say to accept this entropy like it's a trophy.
They say that the only peaceful way is obedience and conformity.

Steal our freedom by making slavery sound normal.
Steal our humanity by making wars sound normal.
Steal our humility by making materialism sound normal.

Deep down, we know who we are.
Deep down, we are fighting to wake up.
Deep down, we are already on our way back to ourselves.

Through dreams, I travel to the past, present, and future.
Through dreams, I travel to the multiverse of my inner
and outer realm.
Through dreams, I find infinity, eternity, and my reality.

Nemesis

Don't think too much, I tell myself;
the candles flicker as my dragons guard me.
I wonder if they are guarding me from the world, or the world from me;
I surrender to the tower I'm locked in and give in to fear.

Then the little yellow-and-blue light of the candle tells me:
'You talk like you are on a battlefield,
and smile carefree like you are in a garden.
Caught in the crossfire of the battle between your self-doubts and duties,
you create your own burden.

'Why don't you come out of your self-imposed amnesia?
Why don't you remember that you are the pain and the panacea?
This tower of darkness is of your own design;
come out already—it's time.

'In being invincible, you found no growth,
so you chose to become vulnerable.
To evolve into you,
you tore yourself into two.

You against You,
because the enemy outside is no match for you.
And you became your own Nemesis.

'The dark side of you welcomed and harboured fear,
to understand it and to explore the depth of your own power.
But you lost your equilibrium in the process and forgot
that it was you who opened the gates for the virus of fear.
You forgot that the Nemesis isn't your doubts or fears;
you forgot that the Nemesis is You.
You gave power to doubts by believing in them;
you gave existence to fears by surrendering to them.
And it's only you that can dispel the dragons of doubts and face
the illusions of fear.

'You are your own Nemesis,
and now it's time to wake up in this climate crisis.
The forests are on fire—wildlife is burning.
The air we breathe is poisoning.
The sea ice is shrinking and the glaciers are melting.
The oceans are warming and the coral reef is bleaching.
The planet we call home is hurting.
You don't have the luxury of overthinking.
It's time to act.
And your actions will drive away your doubts.

'It's time to call the Nemesis for the last duel;
defeat yourself to win.
It's time to become one within.
Break your own rule.

'Train the dragons that entrap you to help you explore the world.

Don't let them hide you from the world or yourself.'

False Spring

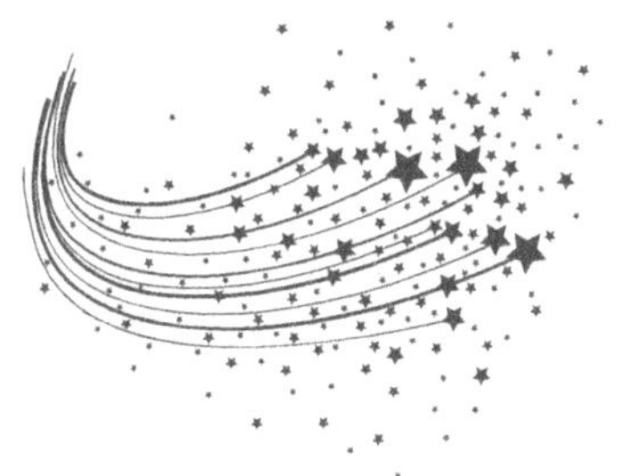

I knew that you were just a shiny chandelier, pretending to be the moon.

But still, a little part of me wanted to believe in the good in you.

So when you arrived, with white plastic flowers in the middle of a snowy winter,

I wanted to believe that you were the Spring.

But that's the thing about a False Spring—

you coax the caterpillar out of its cocoon before its time;

you brazenly make the buds believe that it's warm and safe to bloom in the frost;

you hypnotize the animals to come out of hibernation when their food is still frozen;

you steal the water from snowpacks and disrupt the entire ecosystem.

You are the epitome of humankind out of sync with their humanity—just like a False Spring is a sign of climate catastrophe.

And, when I climbed out of the black hole, you pushed me—

sanctimoniously, you say,

that you were Godsent to test my resilience.

You say that you are glad I made it out alive.

I say: Of course, I'm faster than light.

Your false warmth desynchronized and awakened me

when I still needed the silent slumber of the winter to heal.

But you didn't know that pain evolves me faster and anger emboldens me.

I was a mismatch like a Snowshoe Hare: that, in the false warmth, prematurely turns its coat brown from white and is left vulnerable to the predators.

But you didn't know that I used my vulnerability to embrace authenticity.

Since you said you were Godsent, I spared your life.

But I threw that God who sent you

into the very abyss you dug for me.

A False Spring's warmth cannot fool us for long.

You cannot keep us in a false vacuum for long—

for it's in the nature of every being to move towards its true state—to ground state.

The false dawn that you brought

will surrender when the true dawn arrives.

The brightest of the chandeliers will become non-existent in that sunlight.

The False Spring will melt away in the first bloom of the True Spring.

In this truth, we come together to restore Nature.

In this pure hope lies our power.

In standing up to protect the things we love lies our humanity.

In unity lies our resilience.

The Truth

Truth is a prisoner enshrouded by
a Sorcerer called the mainstream media.
Truth is the elixir that can redeem us,
but we can't drink it because we are already drunk on the lies of
most of these manipulative media.
We are besotted by the Sorcerer,
while Truth is held captive in a secret Chamber
of Corporations that control this Sorcerer.

Truth can change the fabric of this sick society,
but we are blinded, by the illusion of choice, conjured by toxic
media.
The Sorcerer has us worship criminals and crucify saviours.
The Sorcerer cunningly alters our perception and dictates our
reality.
The Sorcerer spews fake news and scandals to cover up crimes
and distract us from reality.

They rely on fear-mongering to deplete our energy.
And most of us believe that all mainstream media is an Agent of
Truth.
Those who stand up for Truth, we vilify
and call them uncouth.

Now humanity is in a state of paralysis,
but there is a way out of this crisis.
You are the Crusader against the Sorcerer—destined to rescue
Truth.
You can do so by choosing Truth over illusions—act like a
sleuth—sift and winnow.
Investigate before you accept anything—
question everything.

Truth can be bitter,
drink it anyway.
Truth can be harsh,
embrace it anyway.

In the end, the Truth comes out anyway,
with or without you. Don't wait till the end—
because that end will be without you.

Oblivion

I smoke the oblivion and soak the setting sun.
It's not just you who have an addiction.
Sometimes I'm more of me,
and at times, I'm less.
I live scattered in different realities.
My mind, this world can't possess.

I drink imagination and dive into the icy ocean.
It's not just you who have an addiction.
Sometimes I want to be all here,
when you draw the infinity.
Your words are colours.
My mind holds onto this reality.

You are my door—
maybe just another addiction.
Or both.
My fall is your redemption.

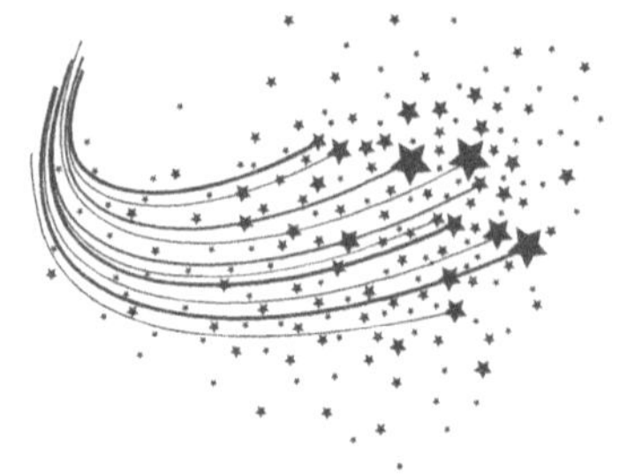

Hush Now

Hush now. I'll weave you a new dream from your tears.
If you feel lost, I'll light your way with stars.
You don't need to know what I do or why I do.
You only need to know that in the darkest dungeons, I'll be at your side.
You may not see me, but you can feel me.

Hush now. Don't stop! The way is through this dark forest.
This darkness didn't come to destroy you.
It came to peel off the layers of worldly constructs from your skin.
The darkness came to heal you.

You cry and think it's your coffin, but it's the chrysalis.
This is not your death but apoptosis.

Learn to be brave on your own.
From this darkness, you have to come out on your own.
Learn to protect yourself first and not to depend on anything or anyone.
From this conundrum, you have to extract the lessons on your own.

I learned the hard way that sometimes my assistance can
unwittingly turn into interference,
and further delay you from your destination.
My absence is not my indifference.
I learned the hard way that sometimes I can help
by not helping.
My silence is not my ignorance.

This is your path, your test.
On this path, I can only guide you
and show you that those colossal clouds are not concrete.

Hush now. You have a journey to complete.
Hush now, I'm with you.

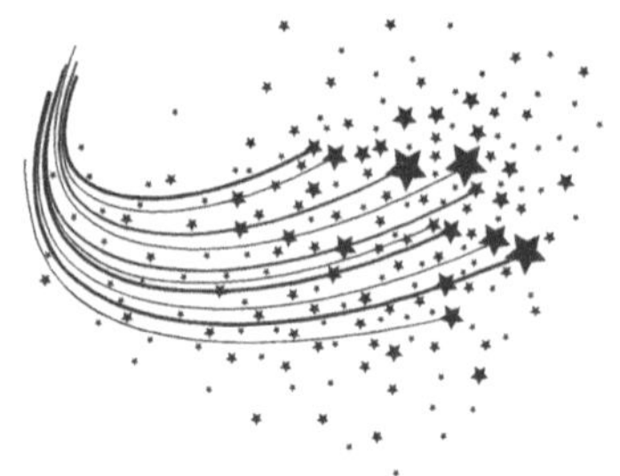

Wild Wind

Wind wind, the way you uncannily
make my hair dance, even when my
head is heavy with thoughts—it's like
you are mocking me when I take life
too seriously.
Like you are reminding me to see the
humour hidden in the journey.
Teach me that, teach me your trick.
It's you, the wild wind, that I want
to mimic.

Majestic Mountains

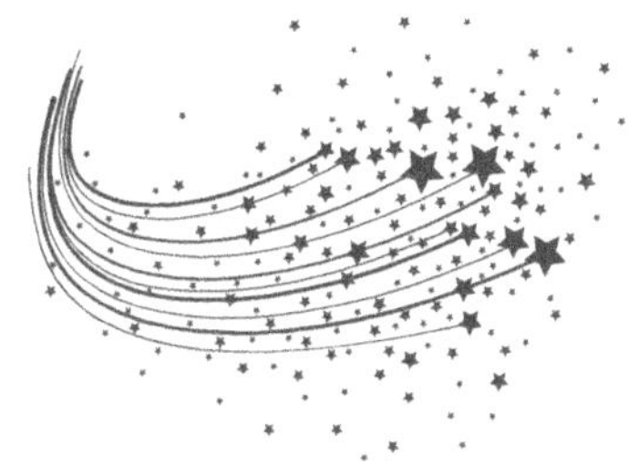

Majestic mountains tell me the stories of travellers
—of conquerors and liars.
They say, There will be a time when you'll lose your ground.
In a world of constant flux, nothing is fixed.
But some things can be constant;
it's your valour—
your Nature.
That, you can always choose.
Who you are and who you want to be—
it's never a chase of a wild goose.
It's no myth.
It's your truth.
And you can always rise, no matter how hard you fall.
Like us, you'll be standing tall—
with us.
We guide you.
Protect you.
You are never alone.
We always talk.
Listen.

A Smile is a Poem

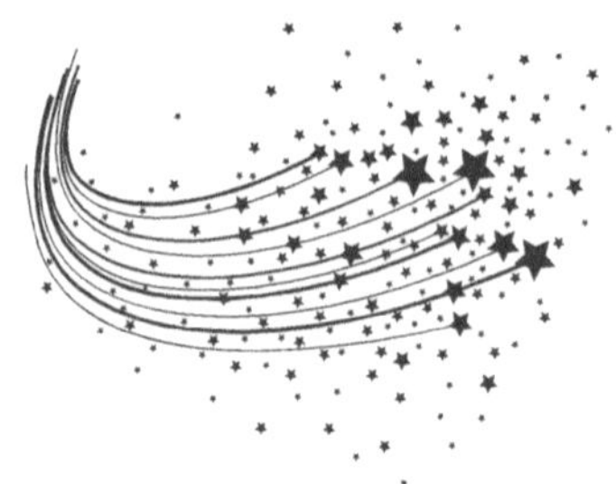

The world seems to run so fast sometimes
—maybe we forget to breathe.
Stuck in a routine or an infinite loop;
then everything feels empty.
We doubt even our own sanity.
Most of us hide it with a smile—no one knows what is beneath.

That absent-minded smile gets reciprocated
by a stranger on the street.
Like silent telepathy,
awakening empathy.
That smile, somehow, makes the bitter air sweet.

A smile is a poem that, without any philosophy,
without any metaphor or simile,
without any rhyme or reason,
shows us we are One—
in pain, in being lost, in being found, in joy.
A smile is a poem that, without a word—
says everything one needs to hear.
A smile is a poem that, without a touch—
connects the hearts.

A smile is a poem that, without a sound—
makes the most beautiful music.

A smile is a poem that tells us—we may be playing different instruments but singing the same song.

Moments

Staring out of the window, lost in thoughts—
I smile, reminiscing the time I did
something silly.
Painting my dreams, I spill colour
on my favourite clothes.
I like the design the spilt
colours made inadvertently.
I sigh—in that moment, I'm Me.

Dancing in the wild, with no plans;
I create the path as I walk—the stars guide me.
I know: not flesh, blood, or bones,
but these moments are Me.

And at times, when troubles show up at my door,
like dust devils rising out of nowhere, I
keep these moments in my heart.
These indelible moments are the bullet points of my whole being.
One small memory of a moment will remind me of another
and show me that I'm bigger
than everything that tries to make me forget who I am.

Wild Fall Flower

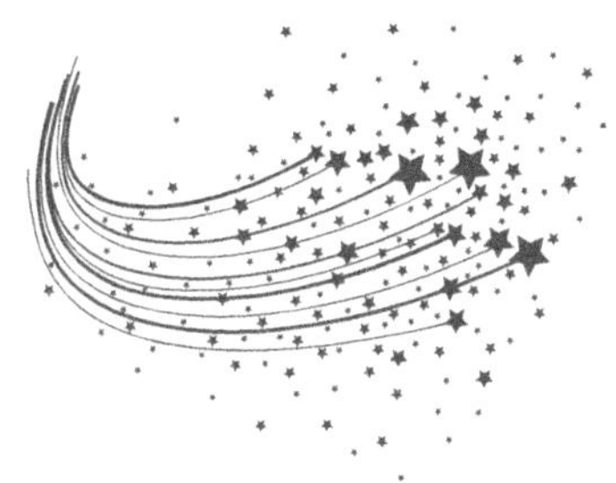

I sent you a message on a wild fall flower.
And I frolicked in the woodland as I waited for a reply.
I watched the autumn leaves fly, like yellow butterflies, in
the blue sky.
Then, after a long wait, the Flower came back with no answer.

The Flower whispered, 'Messages sent on me can be read only by
those
who can see the beauty in the fall,
who can rise from ashes—a brave soul,
who adores the thorns as much as the Rose.'

Quiet displeased with the Flower, I plead,
'What about one more chance?'
The Wild Fall Flower whispered again, 'This will be an endless
dance.
A weed weakens the growth of the grass, let it go, or you will
bleed.'

Morosely I ask, 'Is it not a sign of lack of strength to give up so
easily?'
The Wild Fall Flower sighed, 'Clinging is what lowers your
strength.
Don't get down from your wavelength.
If you want to fly, then fly freely.'

The Flower caressed my hair and stayed there.
It said sleepily, 'Letting go is the purest form of prayer.
Letting go is the true sign of your inner power.'
The Wild Fall Flower then fell asleep on my hair.

$\mathcal{B}rave$

You say with a heavy heart
that you are broken.
You don't hide your darkness,
you face it—
own it.
You shine like a meteor shower even in your brokenness.
To me, you are a mesmerizing mess.

You face your pain like you face your fears.
They may ridicule you,
call you weak.
They have no idea how you fight
your demons alone.
Yet you smile like a ruler on a throne.

Beauty is incorporeal.
It's something to be felt.
They may call you weird or unsightly, but you still make others
feel beautiful.
You don't pretend to be something else or perfect.

To me, that is beauty and courage—the true self that you reflect.

They soil their own face trying to belittle you.
Yet you stand in grace—
a grace that is fire.
You think you are broken, but you are wrong.
To me, you are strong.

And you always try to believe me, even when it's hard.
I'm the voice inside your heart—
the voice that keeps reminding you who you truly are.
All the worlds you can save.
To me, you are Brave.

Don't Fix Me

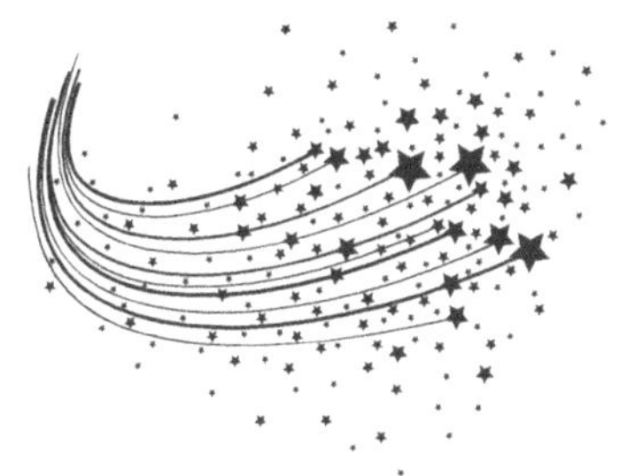

Did you ask the deserts if they want to be green?
Greenery is your idea of perfection.
Did you think before thawing the sea ice to water?
Blind development is your idea of perfection.

Don't fix me,
I am Nature. I can fix
and heal myself.
Just don't interfere and intoxicate me.
I nurtured human beings and gave them a chance to thrive.
This planet is home, equally, to all life.

But now, humanity is infected with hubris
and think they are the most powerful and ultimate.
The dinosaurs thought that too,
and when they crossed the limit,
all I did was call an asteroid.
And as I said, I can heal and fix myself,
so don't be a disease on me.

My silence is not acquiescence.
My love for you is not a weakness.
You know when I speak, Tsunamis and Volcanoes are my
mouthpieces.
And when I react, I won't save the good and punish the bad;
all will be wiped.
To save everything, you must all stand together as one.

I am hurt and damaged, but I can still fix myself.
So you have but little time
to let me heal.
Look at Chernobyl.

Don't fix me, just let me be,
and I can still forgive you.
Or I will burn with you, and like always, I'll fix myself.

Papercut

No, I'm not angry with you,
I'm angry at myself.
After all the battles I fought,
after all the greatest gladiators I defeated—
it wasn't a sword that wounded me this badly.
I'm angry at myself that I let a paper cut me so deeply.

Legacy: An Ode to Ladakh

In the clamour of the crowd going deranged,
hold onto the valiant values bequeathed on you
in the dance of the Black-Necked Crane.
The dance that taught us grace and humility,
causes ripples and pacifies the world,
through our culture and tradition for eternity.
We don't follow the crowd.
We are the children of the celestial cold desert.
In our simplicity lies our majesty.
This is our legacy.

In their false narrative of a naive picture painted of us, that is
untoward—
hold onto your own experience and intuition,
like the sagacious Snow Leopard.
The essence of stillness instilled in us by the elusive ghost of the
mountains teaches us to draw wisdom from innocence and
embrace solitude.
We show the world that innocence is not ignorance.
Even if we get led astray, we can always return to benevolence.
Our innocence is not a liability.
This is our legacy.

The surreality of a single sunbeam saving us from a grim future
turns into reality as we hold onto our faith in ourselves. One is
enough.
Stand alone, and be a loner like the Himalayan Brown Bear,
and look for purpose instead of company.
Like the sparkling stars in the night—far apart, and yet we shine
together.
When the time comes, we also know how to stand in unity.
No matter who you are, you have the power to protect this
paradise;
our homeland Ladakh—the land of high passes.
This is your reality.
This is your legacy.

You are the braveheart who drinks the divine water
that falls from the mystic Mouth of the Lion—*Singey Khabab*.
You reflect the grandeur of the glaciers in your gait.
Your shine is conspicuous even when you feel weak—like the
sublime snow peaks glowing in the moonlight.
You blend in with the surroundings and adapt to extreme
conditions, like the resilient Red Fox.
You are shy and yet clever, like the gallant Antelope and
the placid Ibex.
You can be both homely and wild, like the Yak; never ordinary.
So don't forget your history.
Don't let go of your legacy.

Raid the Mountains

Your heart aches for adventure, and your mind
misses the wilderness.
So you decide to raid the mountains,
drunk on some vain idea of an adventure.
Then audaciously off-road vehicles on the wetlands and
meadows;
jeopardize the already endangered birds,
and crumple the ground-nesting species—destroying their
burrows.
You call it fun and don't mind if Nature pays the cost.
If that's your idea of an adventure, then you are lost.

To experience real bliss, learn to respect all species—
from the rare black-necked crane to the abundant bees.

Your loud vehicles cause unrest to the wildlife, and your mindless
activities leave a high carbon footprint.
The noise disturbs the hibernation process of
vulnerable species;
while you litter, waste scarce water—completely disregarding and
disrespecting the indigenous way of life.
The dust and pollution hamper the growth process of herbs and
plants;
raising the temperature and causing faster glacial melt.

Superficial things that are insipid for a traveller are intrepid for a
shallow tourist.
You try to show that you are fearless by making the wildlife afraid.
If that's your idea of an adventure, then your life is a charade.

To maintain the fragile ecosystem, we need all flora and fauna.
Be it the huge Himalayan Brown Bear, the innocent Blue Poppy,
the Wild Iris or the small Pika.

You put unsustainable pressure on Nature for greed,
or to fill the emptiness that you feel with all the wrong things;
it's a sign that you need healing.
Healing is not simple; its path is thorny and strange.
Instead of taking that path, you prefer to chase phantasm of
pleasure.
Healing takes time for Nature as well, for it takes years for
degraded habitat to recover.
You find pleasure in hurting Nature.
If that's your idea of an adventure, then you have no future.

To experience real thrill, we must practice being carbon neutral.
It's the only adventure that is not ephemeral.
If you were born in the mountains and yet forgot your roots,
and made a mistake of putting your homeland at risk,
then forgive yourself and turn back—it's not too late.
Don't feel small if you fall for the false gleam of a glamorous
desire
that made you ignore the tears of the blue sky.
Forgive yourself and remember that we can never be in bondage.
We can still protect our Natural Heritage.
Don't take those glitters for gold in the name of progress.

If that's your idea of an adventure, then neither you nor Nature
can convalesce.

To be on a true adventure, protect the Natural Heritage;
understand you are a part of it and break the
ignorance's cage.

When the mountains call,
don't answer by raiding it.
The strength of the mountains is in your spirit, and
that's why you hear its call.
The rugged brown mountains are calling you to teach you
courage.
The enchanting colourful mountains are calling you to bestow in
you—placidness.
And when you crave adventure,
don't find it as a tourist;

be with the mountains like you belong there already.
Then the Mountains will show you that
you are the adventure you crave,
and the wilderness runs in your blood.
Realize it and free yourself.

The Hero

Mountains taught the Hero dignity,
but he was too weak to learn it.
Now he has power, and it didn't take talent
but sycophancy to earn it.

But obsequiousness only gets one so far.
Now the facade is falling.
Truth rips off the mask from the face of the pseudo-hero
eventually.
And now the people can see
how this capricious Hero vacillates unapologetically.

Real Heroes gave up their lives for the cause
that this Hero is abusing and corrupting.
He mixed poison in the honey of hopes.
He pretends to hear the pleas while silently
dissipating dissenters.
He tries to sell lies as if the people are
ignorant and blind;
as if his treachery is a destiny that people
are inextricably intertwined.
The people of the mountains believed that
this Hero broke all curses of the land.
But now they are awake from the spell of this Hero Worship.

Now they ask the Hero: Is this the legacy of your leadership?
Generations will talk about all inflicted hardship.

Power is a fickle friend—it's evanescent.
One day, it flashes like medals on the chest of a champion
And the other day, you are just an obedient hound, tied on the
gates of those in power.
You can still be the Hero that the people believed.
With integrity, you can still lead.
Or else, in the end, you will be devoured by your own misdeed.
It wasn't curiosity that killed the cat. It was greed.

UFO

I have been flying haplessly like a dead leaf
blown by the autumn wind.

My battle wounds look surreal to others, like
the colours of the fall.

I have been floating aimlessly in the space like
a broken object

in the aftermath of a storm.

My shattered pieces pique curiosity in others like an unidentified
flying object.

Must I always be dead or broken to be beautiful?

Overthinking

Let me try to paint a picture of my overthinking—
I don't know if it's fear out of anger
or anger out of fear.
Sinking in an endless ocean
or a drop of tear.
It's like I want to want;
the kind of greed,
that will make me want to keep living.
But at the same time, one by one, my desires cease;
overthinking is my favourite disease.

With overthinking, I can consume hell in a sip of a thought.
But I can also build a paradise when my overthinking is
subsumed, with an embrace of imagination.

SOS

My mind talks a lot, and my heart barely listens.

So I ran away from both and hid in an empty space and sent an S.O.S to them.

I will only return when they save our ship by working together.

Escape Velocity

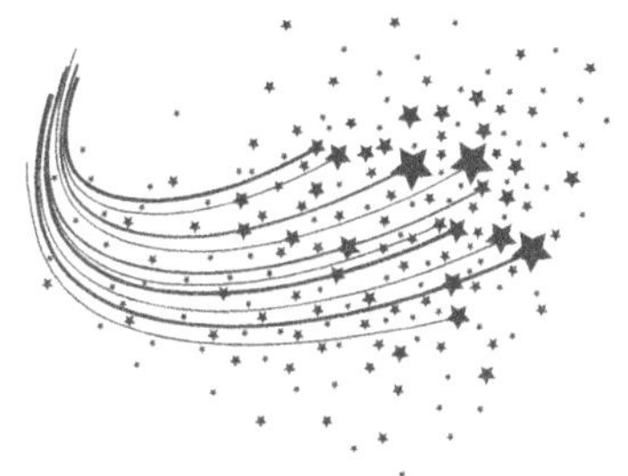

Even when you know that there is a pot of gold
at the end of the rainbow, you call it a myth
just because you can't touch it.
You keep looking for external help and approval,
and if you don't find it, you turn taciturn and tacitly
believe that it wasn't meant for you.
You drown with your own permission—
you lose the way under your own direction.
The inaction, capitulation, the silence
is permission.
To find freedom, you have to escape first
from the things that steal your identity.
Escape the grip of your own insecurity.
Get to your escape velocity.
Be like a rainbow that doesn't follow the rules
of black and white.
The process will be slow and painful,
but it will turn the journey more colourful.
You don't need permission to dream, to fly, to win.

Indifference

All the bridges that I built for you, I won't hesitate
to burn it.

My indifference is worse than my anger, so don't earn it.

An Ode to Snowfall

Snow falls quietly—
as if it loves everything unconditionally.
It engulfs the noise of the world
as I sit by the fireplace, curled.

The snowflakes gleam and glide gracefully like an ethereal
dancer.
Their mystic music that only my heart could hear
coaxes me out like a snake charmer.
Hypnotised, I swirl out of my hibernation.
It's snowing, and it breaks the spell of an unending rumination.

It's snowing, and the sound of it,
crunching under my feet
is disenthralling.
The world feels like a bearable place to live when it's snowing.
It's snowing without knowing the magic it's unfolding.

Beautiful

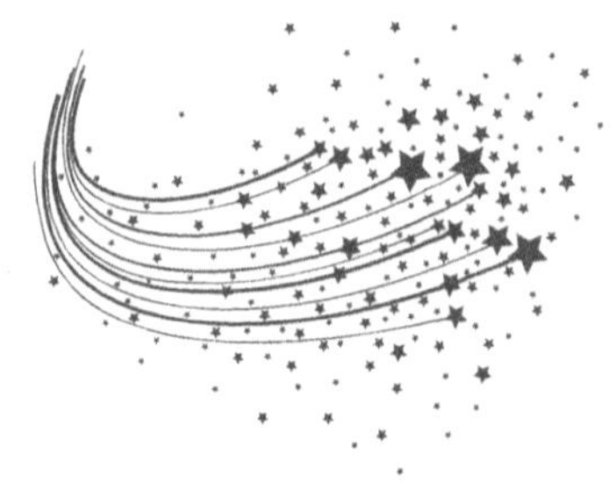

I don't want to be beautiful like,
wear a crown,
talk of the town.
I want to be beautiful like
the mountains and the seas
that brings peace.
I want to be beautiful like Truth—
that is ugly if you don't want it;
that sets you free if you still choose it.
I want to be beautiful like the mirror of the Universe—
that reflects the beauty of everyone;
that reminds others of the beauty in them.
I want to be beautiful like beauty—
that is Love.

3

Equilibrium

So they asked me if I believed in Love.
I said, 'How can I not believe in myself?'

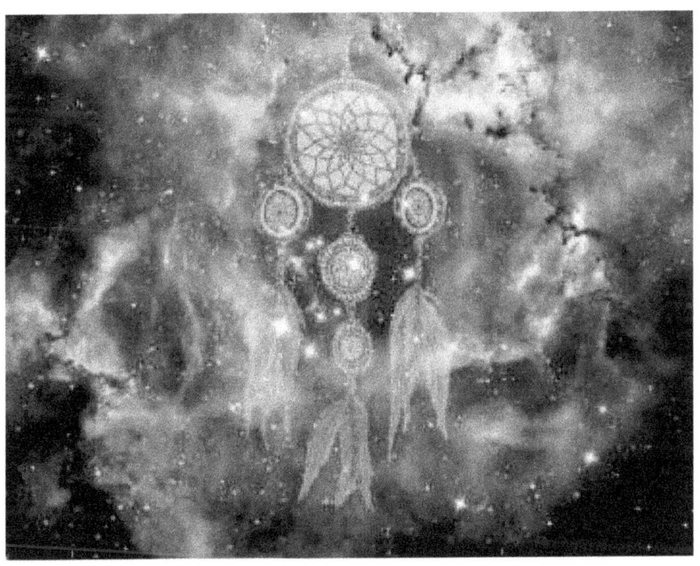

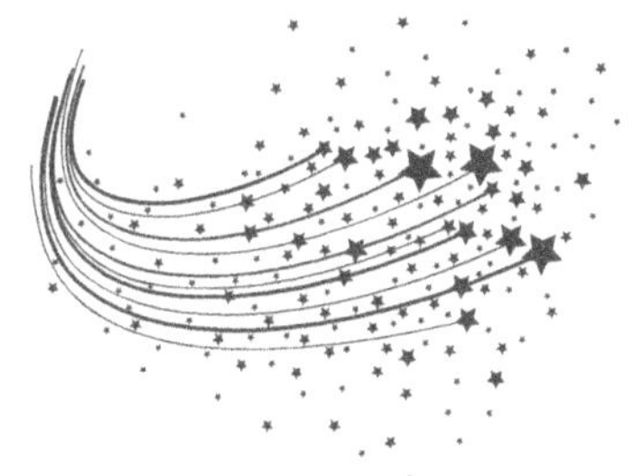

Phoenixes and Fairies

When I tell you about my pain
and how I overcame it—you call me a Phoenix.
Oh, your sweet talks!
When I forgive your mistakes
and tell you to live with integrity—you call me a Fairy.
Oh, your sweet talks!

When you try to reduce me to a pretty little thing,
I know you are patronising.
You try to box me in your mind's limited understanding.
I confess I find that amusing.
You try to place on my head the crown of your control,
I know how weak you are feeling.
You call me strong and yet passively try to make
me feel weak.
I admit I tolerated more than I should in
trying to be forgiving.

What you don't know
is that I woke up long ago.
The vultures think that the sleeping lion is dead.
But it's just too lazy to get out of its bed.

Your sweet talks—I could turn it into poison on your tongue.
You witnessed that my joy can bring a serene snowfall,
then how could you not know that my anger can call an
avalanche.

Take your sweet words and phoney affection—
it's nauseating.
All this time, I learnt to be on my own—
now you know that phoenixes and fairies don't mind flying alone.

Strange Thing

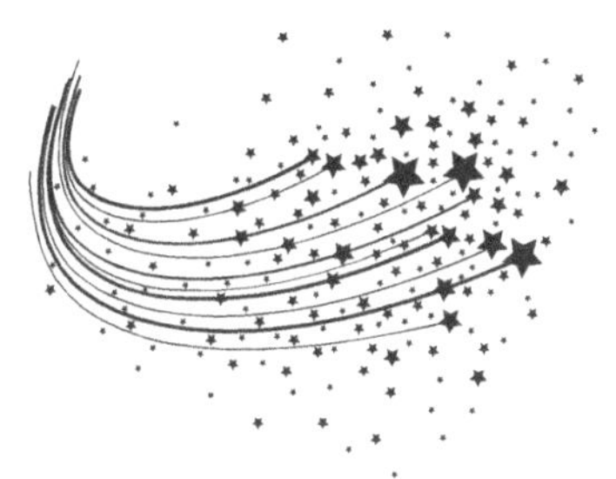

Superciliously, you say, All good things come to an end.
You keep saying what everybody says.
You keep conforming and yet think that you are different.
You say that you think out of the box.
I say, Get rid of the box.

Keep your limiting thoughts to yourself.
Don't impose them on me.
So you believe that good things come to an end;
well, hear my truth—
I'm not a good or a bad thing that will end.
I'm a Strange thing
and I'm here to stay.

Be a Bee

Even when humanity is leading to anomie—
we, the bees, still fight to sustain our colony.
People search for their purpose,
but we are born with it innately.
Our work is divine for us, which reflects
in our elixir of honey.
Our work is selfless, and that's why we fill this world with
an abundance of foods, fruits, and flowers.

The more you take, the more you choose gluttony instead of
gratitude.
It's in our nature to be giving with fortitude.
Is solely taking with apathy the nature of humanity? You take
unabashedly with certitude.
Poisonous pesticides are proclaimed safe for profit and used in
alarming magnitude.
And now, slowly poisoned, we, the bees who were born with a
purpose—
can't even navigate our way back to hives.
We are declining and facing Colony Collapse Disorder.
Do you know how painful it is to lose our
purpose and family?
Do you know how dreadful it is to be unable to find the way back
to our home—our colony?

You can still save us by practising ethical beekeeping and
restoring impoverished habitats.
You can still save humanity by working together to sustain this
world—just as the bees work together to sustain their colony.

When our habitat is healthy, so shall be our queen.
If you start to nurture Nature instead of greed,
then together,
we can defeat all viruses that deform our wings;
for us, it's the
Varroa mite, and for you, it's your unsustainable practices.

It's time humanity learns harmony from the bees.
It's time to have the determination to do something
bigger than yourself—like the pollinators.
It's time to show your loyalty to Nature and thrive—like
the sedulous bees loyal to their queen and the beehive.
Let's be in a bee mentality.
Let's be a bee.

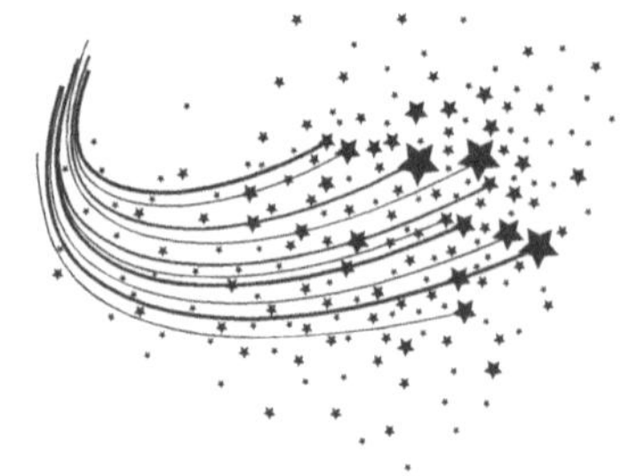

Perfect Paradise

You wonder why I chose the tough path
when you showed me the easy way.
You wonder why I preferred to live in the
harsh desert when you offered me paradise.
Over me, hollow comforts hold no sway.
Well, for me, I never liked easy anyway.
Keep your perfect paradise;
I would rather burn in my real hell
and rise as my true self.

Know Where You Belong

Know where you belong.
You cling to people, who don't understand you,
just to fit in a mad society.
They make you feel ugly, and you believe it.
You accept being the ugly duckling even when you know you are
different because you are a swan.
You gobble up your own individuality just to feel normal.

Know where you belong.
Choose your people; a philosopher will call you a thinker—
the night will call you the moon.
But if you choose the herd, they will call you lost if you don't
follow their path.
And in a lost world, you question your own existence.
Your heart whispers the truth, and you pretend to be deaf
to find acceptance.

Know where you belong.
And if you still don't know where you belong,
then go to yourself.
The silence in your heart will scream your identity,
and the noise in your head will form a stairway to the sky—

where you are the ruler.
You belong to your eyes that twinkle with dreams.
You belong to your spirit that blooms with colours.
You belong to yourself.

September Snow

You were a September snow—too little, too early.
I wasn't ready for the cold, blustering wind
you brought along.
The cold wind collapsed the castle of dreams I built.
Those dreams were fragile and sensitive, like my heart.
But the will to save them was as strong as my mind.
So I watered those dreams back to life and
rebuilt them stronger.
I closed my windows and shut the door on you.
I couldn't bear the unwarranted cold.
I couldn't enjoy that untimely snowy day—as much as I love the
snowfall.

September snow—too little, too early,
too inconsistent.
A little here,
a little there,
and half empty.
Ill-timed. I have no time.
No time to welcome half-hearted guests
in the pure castle of my dreams.

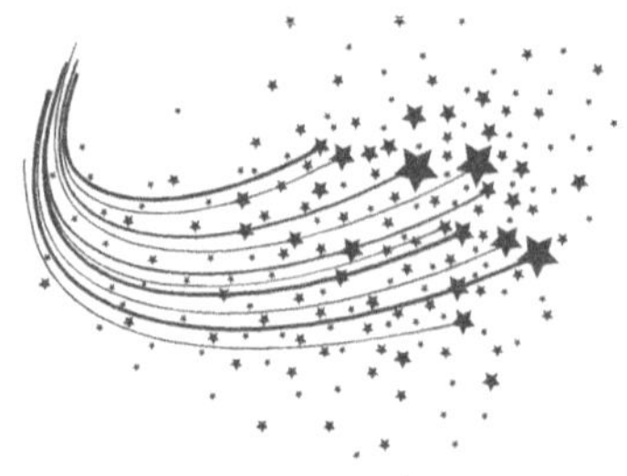

Joy

Traversing the cold desert,
I stop to taste the sour sea buckthorn berry
as the sun loves my hair and skin to golden tawny.
I squint my eyes, relishing the refreshing tangy.
Joy finds me, even in the dry dust and hurt.

Joy is a gem that is innately yours.
It can come to you as something spectacular or as a silly little
thing;
in a sip of hot butter tea on a chilly morning—
as a gust of wind fragrant with a forgotten yearning.
Joy will find you even if you close all doors.

Joy is your eternal companion.
Distinguishing between true and false—your
eyes are tired.
So close your eyes and open your heart.
Let your eyes rest and look through your heart.
There you'll see that scarcity is only an illusion.
Go to joy—don't wait for it to return.
Look in your heart when things seem tenebrous.
There you will see joy, unfurling beauty and healing like a rare
snow lotus.
It's all within—all you have to do is to focus.
Joy is waiting for you to return.

Birds of Paradise

Beguiled by the song of a bird,
I followed it to the woods.
There it perched atop a branch of a willow tree;
the sonorous song of that bird of paradise
ameliorated my sinking heart, and I sat beneath the tree,
admiring the bird's bizarre beauty.
It looked like a bedizened bride, and yet, looked tranquil and
simple,
with plumage of iridescent sheen and a purple crown.
The serene song made me fall asleep.
Suddenly, I heard someone cry—
'Wake up, wake up!'
I opened my eyes
and saw the bird weeping.

'You can talk!' astonished, I exclaimed.
The bird said, 'Yes. But to others, it will sound like an
unintelligible bird song.
I sing about the looming death
that hovers above us—

extinction that took the Unicorns, Phoenixes, and Mermaids.'

'But they are mythical creatures.' I replied.
The bird said, 'What's more mythical? A horn in the middle of a
horse's head—
or the purple crown on my head?
—the tooth of a Narwhal or the long teeth of Mammoths?

'They already call us the Birds of Paradise—
already we are otherworldly.
Just how long do you think
until we become chimerical?
So I came to warn humanity.
If you don't act on time,
soon it will be the turn of humankind to go extinct.
Then a new species will come
And, if the humans are lucky,
they will find the fossil of your kind.
If not, you'll be mythical just like us—
living only in tales and imagination.
Humanity will be the New Unicorn
of the next species.'

Reflection

I can make you feel alive,
and I can also be your death.
Marie Curie—
I am your discovery.
I am your dream—your nightmare.
I am not an imposter,
Frankenstein—
I am your Monster.

The clutter grows on and on in a pile.
There is no stop to your denial.
Keep blowing your trumpet
while you shove the dirt inside the carpet.
You won't fly until you fall from the edge.
You can't fix what you don't acknowledge.

Nothing to panic,
I am your Titanic.
The poison could be you—it's unthinkable.
Don't think your ship is unsinkable.
You fear me, but I am your reflection.
In the mirror, you see a forest-eating demon;
who slaughters and abuses animals and causes deforestation.

You feel the impact of the greenhouse gas emissions
and yet support corporate greed and political chicanery—
even if it results in the loss of biodiversity and climate emergency.
The forests are the protectors of the planet,
but for industrial meat, you burn it down with no regret.

You run away from me, but I am your freedom—
your complete reflection.
You have this illusion of separation.
And now, you are about to reach the event horizon.
When you harm nature, you sabotage yourself.
Face me and fix yourself.
You get what you give—
it's a souvenir that you must receive.

I am the souvenir standing on your door as a wildfire.
I am the Monster, you sire.
I am the discovery that can take your life.
You have to heal yourself from this internal strife.
Fact or fiction,
I am your retribution and redemption.

Acknowledge your faults and fix them.
The people that you care about lives in the same realm.
Before your loved ones open the door—
before the point of no return—everything you must restore.

Too Sweet

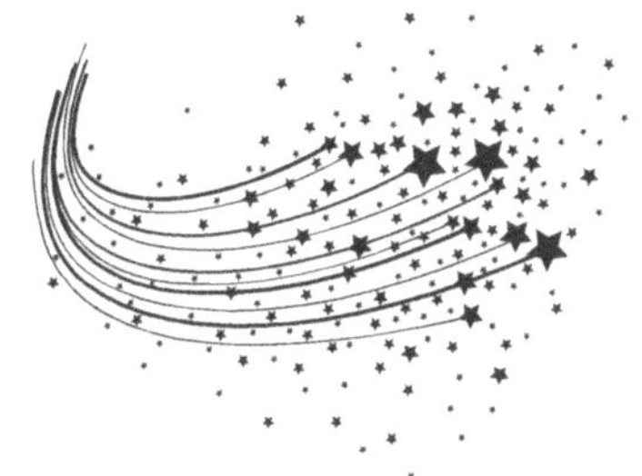

This is not the first time I turned away from a battlefield.

It wasn't because I was scared, but because I knew it wasn't my war to fight.

My old scars are the witness and turning back from this decoy—my wisdom.

And now that I'm letting go of the thing that I wanted the most;

they come and say that the grapes are sour.

I'm letting go because I realised that the grapes are too sweet and sickening.

My grief is the witness and fair detachment—my power.

Equanimity

What is power?

You let the illusory dance of power hypnotise you, even
when you promised yourself that you would keep
your soul unsullied.

But what you think is power are merely echoes of it.

And you chose to chase those echoes of power—hoping
it will complete your identity;

hoping it will lead you to a place that you desire to be.

What is happiness?

You languidly dream of a perfect paradise where
there is only happiness.

And you chase happiness like you chase power.

But happiness is only one flavour in the infinite
seasonings of emotions.

One cannot be happy to be happy all the time, just like one
can't savour sweetness every time.

True power is hidden, like a rare ruby in equanimity.

True purpose is not to find happiness—it is to find
equanimity through self-discovery.

You can be so much more than just happy—embrace all
emotions.

Your paradise is right here right now, and you are the creator.

Equanimity is the balance of all emotions;

to be equanimous is to be magnanimous with your power.

Equanimity enkindles the calm in the chaos and
illumines the

dark caverns of the mind.   ~ 73 ~

Equanimity is your armour on the path to reach power,
and power is you.

Equanimity is the endless reservoir of happiness
already within you.

Gold

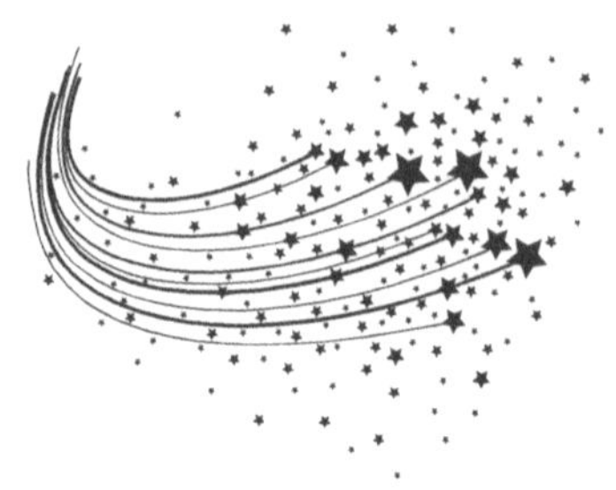

Don't know what to call this—your ignorance
or that you are too bold.
To an alchemist, you show off your gold.
I collapsed and formed under the gravity
of my own thoughts—more times
than the amount of breath that you could ever take in your
existence.
Don't try to woo a wild thing in a zoo.

The Tale of Four Seasons-
Shades of Autumn

I tip-toed on the dewdrops,
took a lift from the fireflies,
climbed the clouds
and coaxed the sun,
to form a shade of fire and fall.

Entranced the earth to create a scent out of the fallen leaves—
that will remove the stench of
preconceived notions.
Bewitched the leaves to fall in such a motion,
like shedding old emotions.

Won the warmth of the wind
to carry that scent to you.
I know you are suffocating; it's not your fault.
It's the cold spell of perpetual petrification,
moulded by blind self-justification—
to say, all is pointless.
The shade of Yellow yawned as it absorbed
the tears from your weary eyes.
I know you are tired of seeing corpses

who walk like living beings.
Humanoid—
that you cannot avoid.

Here, a bit of shade of Orange
that I quietly stole when the sun was setting
to lift your spirits.
I know you want to fall.
Don't.
Because you don't want to follow anymore.
So don't.

Take this shade of Red—
the colour of power and passion
that runs in your blood.
I know you want to stop copying the notes from a system that
promises to deliver freedom.
Flame your fire and be done.

Do fall like the tree
that sheds only the leaves, not itself.
Do follow Nature to witness the beautiful irony
that, when you copy Nature, you become original.
I know you feel that your strength is infinitesimal.
Just keep walking, and you'll reach.

It's for the time to teach,
as this message is subliminal.

Leave the leaves now,
no matter how alluring they look.

Yellow, red, orange and strange.
Autumn is the Pied Piper that came to lead you out.
It's a healing hypnotizer
that you must follow without a doubt.

Create your inner sanctum
in the Shades of Autumn.

The Tale of Four Seasons- Wistful Winter

When Winter woke up, everything was gone;
no flowers,
no leaves on the trees—
Winter felt all alone.
Even most of the birds had flown away to warmer places.
Most people had left as well.
And as Winter tried to make sense of it all—
Damn this Winter!
—it only heard the curses.

Winter felt forlorn and sickly.
Feeling unwanted and unloved,
Winter whimpered, and it made the sky overcast.
The grey sky made Winter feel lonelier, and Winter started to cry
bitterly.
The tears of Winter turned into snow.
Slowly, Winter opened its eyes and saw the shimmering view.
On its icy skin, felt the gleaming tears bedew.
Winter felt an emotion inside aglow.
Winter said, 'I can illuminate the sombre with splendour.
My art is my friend—I'm not an anomaly.

My work is my company.'
Realizing this, Winter smiled in fervour.
The icy chill froze Winter's fatalistic ego.
The clouds cleared, and the sun shone dazzlingly.
Animals and children came out to play in awe;
the gloominess bloomed into joviality.

Winter watched as people threw snowballs at each other
and built snowmen and snow castles.
Halcyon Winter beamed with the harmony it helped create.
Then a sudden realization dawned—like winning a thousand
battles.
Winter said, 'Only if I create my art effectively,
Spring, Summer, and Autumn can emanate.
Although we cannot meet,
they will feel me in the glistening water melting down the glaciers.
When I'm gone, my essence will
help them fulfil their duties as my magic lingers.

'I don't have time to feel low,
I've to create all this snow.
So when it's warmer, there is plenty of water
for flowers to bloom, for the grass to be green.
I'll turn my melancholy into fuel to fulfil my dream.'
And all of a sudden, the wind dropped three letters.

The first letter was from Spring.
It said, 'Thank you. I'm sending you the first blossom to remind
you that you are wanted.
So don't be Forgetful Winter.
You are always cherished.'

The second one was from Summer,
It said, 'I got your gift, my dear Wise Winter.
I'm sending you the sweetness of fruits and the scent of flowers to show my gratitude.
Don't be Wistful Winter.
You are loved.'

The last letter was from Autumn.
It said, 'Please accept these amber hues and clear your blues.
Don't be Achromic Winter.
For you can make even stark white colourfully aglitter.
You are not alone.'

Winter no longer felt unwanted,
and thought to itself, 'It's time for me to sleep peacefully.
Like a dream, I will forget all of this again
and on waking up, I'll be in pain
to see that I'm all alone.
I'll cry.
But there is bliss in this ignorance,
for I'll witness the majesty of my magic, always anew,
and find out along the way that I'm loved and never alone.
'The path will be full of agony.
And times will be testing.
But sometimes, pain is a blessing.
And Solitude—the best company.'

The Tale of Four Seasons-
Song of Spring

Wondering with the wind—
the memories that the fragrant breeze brings.
O colours of spring.
I don't stop—I let go.
I'm Life.
I flow.

Singing with the Spring;
only trying to tie a loose string.
O colours of spring.
On my way now.
I'm Death.
I grow.

The Tale of Four Seasons-
The Kiss of Summer

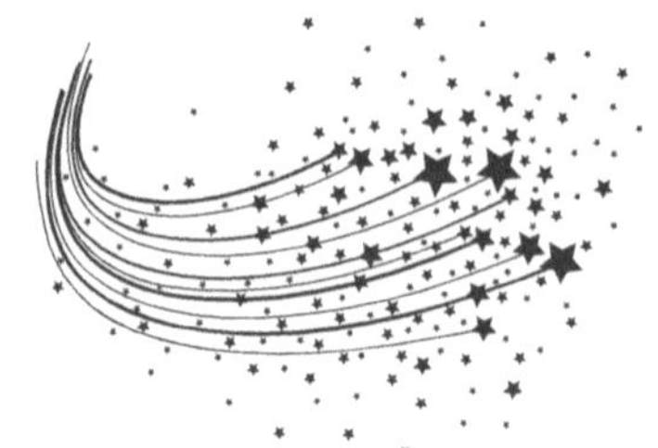

The sunbeams kissed the summer awake.

All you ever dreamed and hoped for is in front of your eyes.

Without knowing the rhyme or reason,

you made it through all the seasons.

Without counting or calculating,

you reached the end of your beginning.

You kept company with the lonely Wistful Winter and learned patience.

You listened to the Song of Spring and earned wisdom.

You survived the fall and found a sanctum in the Shades of Autumn.

And now, the victor found the answer hidden in the Kiss of Summer.

Equilibrium

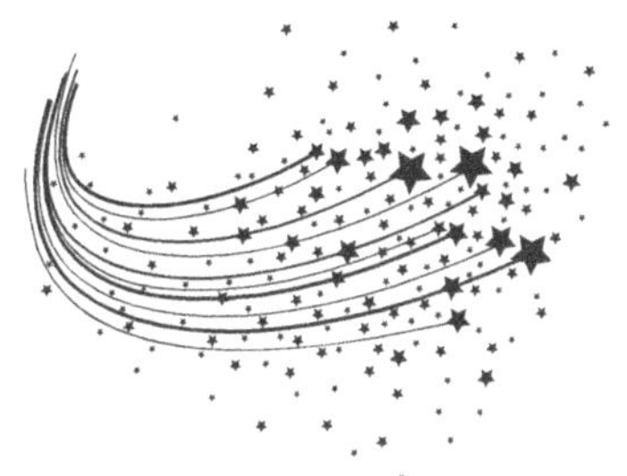

Maybe it's easy to understand for a few.
Nightmares that can't be averted—
truth that can't be reverted.
Seriously, for me, it's nothing new.
It's like I'm playing a game of maze runner;
running on a passage that makes false appear real—
answers, hidden behind a magical veil.
Assuming that I'm afraid, you offer me your dream catcher.
Your intentions, as pure as this dream catcher,
I won't even trade one nightmare.

I space out in time,
and now my coffee has gone cold.
You say, A penny for your thoughts?
I say, It's nothing new.

You think that I'm lost,
but I'm just a silent observer.
It's my pain and pleasure.
I notice everything—

the patterns of butterflies and clouds,
the songs of birds and the screams of doubts.

And in the stupor of this drunkenness,
say it's insanely sane or sanely insane;
as they say—there is a method to the madness.

Maybe it's tough to understand for a few.
This road that I'm walking on has no footprints.
No banners or hints.
Seriously, for me, it's something new.
It's like the joy that only pain could bring;
I can see the ephemeral and the bigger picture.
The answers now don't even matter.
From enthralling experiences, a wisdom spring.
Now I don't look up to you or
ask for solutions anymore.
Out of perplexity, you reveal to me all the secrets
and disclose the correct way.
You tell me that it will save me from delay
I say, I'll find it on my own.

You say, It could take an eternity.
I say, When thoughts are transcendental
poison becomes a potion.
And if Life is all about learning, I don't mind even if it's eternal.

Maybe it's tough and easy to understand for a few
When illusions fail to sway your mind,
chaos will try to make you blind.
And amidst this storm,

the balance you can always find.
Seriously, for me, it's something true—
to live for and to die for.

You ask me, At least let me get you another round of coffee?
I reply, Yeah, that's something you could do for me.
You smile and test me again
and tell me that my truth isn't real.
You say that I live in another world
—that I stay in a dream world.
I say, I live neither in the dream world nor in the real world.
I live in the middle of both.
I stay in Equilibrium.

4

The Big Crunch

*I am the colour of the rainbow and the
darkness of the night.*
Stars are my army, and my power—the sunlight.
Moon is my calm side.
On a snow-storm, I ride.
I am the ruler of the sky.
I am you.

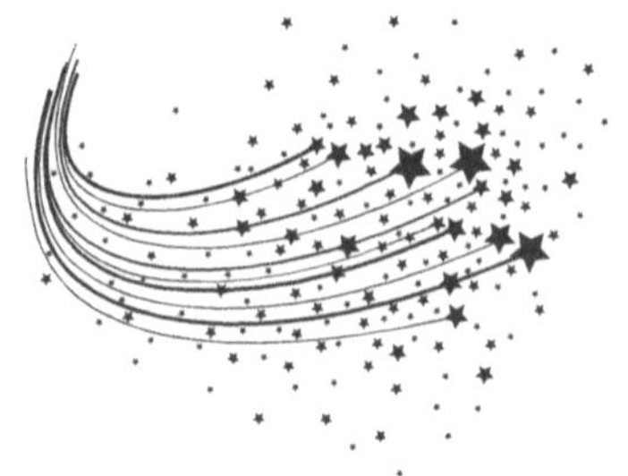

Nobody and Nothing

I spent my life gallivanting in the galaxies,
looking for my lost heart.
I lost my heart when I stopped following it
and followed the crowd instead—
running with the crowd to be somebody and something.
A 'somebody' who people expected me to be but
who I wasn't.
A 'something' that I thought I should be but didn't
want to be.
Now that I have searched every nook and corner
of this universe
for my dear heart, I stand defeated as I find it nowhere.
Then I sat in the 'nowhere', drowning in my own tears
as I cried
with all my being.
My tears then filled the empty space and infiltrated the cosmos,
posing to extinguish the fire of all the Suns.
The threatened Sun then sent me a message on a comet
that ripped open the void with its dazzling light
and said—
'Sit with silence and listen to the song of the oblivion.
Be Nobody and Nothing.
Your tears have already awakened your sleeping heart.

When you dare to be No One, then you create the space and power to be everything.

And then you can choose to be the One who is Infinite—choose to imagine and reimagine the real you.'

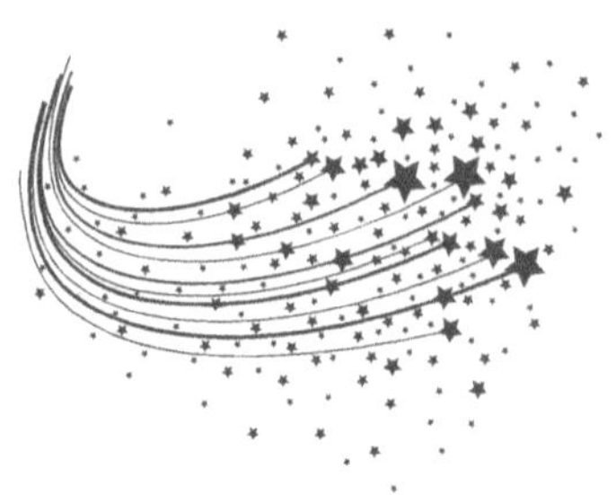

Antidote

Welcome to hell!
It used to be the place you dwell.
You designed it according to the approval of others.
Oh, look at the fancy decor.
Yet you don't feel at 'Home'.

Click here, and click there, watch this, and watch that.
You quench your thirst for knowledge
with random information—
you betray yourself.
Then all you do is compare—
you steal from yourself.

And now, when you finally see the trap, you
want yourself back.
You see, now you have everything, but still, your Palace is always
in a lack.
No matter what you do, it's missing you—
the 'You'—that you edited out according to the trend.
You know the map back to yourself, but you still need the
Antidote to heal
because the poison of comparison is still in you.
Now you set off on an expedition
to find the Antidote.

But you chose a capsized boat
because you haven't stopped seeking validation.
It's a Sisyphean loop—
doomed, like going to war without a troop.

Technology can be all—just a tool, as it is
supposed to be—
a guide that can help us attain the utopia of Technological
Singularity;
but in the process, if we let go of our humanity,
then it can lead us to the dystopia of the same.
It's up to us which side of it we awaken
because we created technology.

Social Media is a three-headed creature like a Chimera.
You only look at the benign goat head and don't notice it can
also breathe fire and delude us.
Why burn when you can use its fire to warm yourself
or to light up the world.

The currency is not the attention of others.
The currency is your attention towards things that matter.
You don't have to go to wars or expeditions to attain real
treasure.
So stop this war within and call back your ships.
The Antidote is already on your lips.
Neither by heaven nor by hell—
the Antidote can be activated by a simple spell
uttered from your lips.
Say, 'I stop and free myself from this slavery of addiction. I
reclaim my life now.
To these illusions, my head will no longer bow.'

Welcome Home!
You took back your throne.
And now you designed your home with myriad colours;
real—laughter, pain, sweet dreams and nightmares.
Now it feels like home.

Violet Flames and Fireflies

(Based on a dream)

It seems that with humankind, we have reached an impasse.

But we believe that the divine flame is in all of us.

We, the fireflies, show this lost world that true light comes from within.

But you are blinded by artificial lights, to our chagrin.

In the gloomiest forests, the fireflies glow and gleam.

We are the beacons of hope and dream.

Magical things can be small and simple.

But this world judges by beauty and power that's superficial.

We are dying.

But you won't reduce your ecological footprint.

We are disappearing.

But you won't take the hint.

We lose our habitat to human whims.

But you callously crush us with foot traffic.

We lose our divine dark to light pollution, chemical pollution—
this is our apocalypse.

But for you, we are mere objects, and you only care if we appear
pleasing for your pictures—your apathy is tragic.

Our language is of light: Violet light calls you back to your
highest frequency and energy.

It's not too late for humanity.

Violet flames and fireflies

call humanity to awaken its inner light before
everything dies.

$Stargazer$

My mind is an explorer,

and my heart is the compass.

Turning the stones hurled on me into snowflakes,

I keep walking, and obstacles on my path transform into soft
snow.

I tread boldly on the fresh snow and make my own mark;

I follow no footprints.

Sleeping by the bonfire with the

lullaby of the crackling fire,

drawing the dreams like a map

and eluding every trap—

the Stargazer stares at the moon

and treats the darkness like a boon.

People mock the Stargazer but, deep down,

hope to get infected by the stardust

that liberated the Stargazer.

So they attack the Stargazer, hoping to get its secret.

The Stargazer, completely indifferent, tells the people:

Why look for a saviour when you are a protector yourself?
Why look for a god when you have the
universe within you?
Why look for a magician when you are
the magic itself?

But the people couldn't believe in such a simple secret,
and thought that the Stargazer is a liar, so they screamed:
Burn this maverick!
Drown in hell!

The Stargazer then shines so brightly,
unfolding the wings made of stars,
and as the Stargazer flies far away, smiles and tells the people:
But alas! You cannot burn the sun and drown the ocean.

Apocalypse

Nascent in the night,
the morbid feelings melt into the morning.
And still, you open your eyes every day,
not surrendering to the apparitions of the dark.
Just how many demons did you defeat last night?
How many times have you thought—this is the End of Me?
And how many times have you thought—this is the Apocalypse?

Slept on it,
cried on it,
or ate on it.

O, the night's nostalgia.
That tiny spark in you
will never let this be the end of you.
The spark, no matter how small it gets,
will never disappear—it's invincible.
The spark is your Spirit.
Trust that inner light.
It's the only thing that's true.
O, the morning's melancholia.
Now that you are adept at the darkness,
the memories don't haunt you anymore.

You even look back at it fondly.
Now, it's a part of your story.
It was the darkness that threw you into your light.
It was the darkness that led you to this Apocalypse.
But this Apocalypse is not the end.
This Apocalypse is the revelation of your truth—
as the curtain falls on the lies.

Masks and people

I wake up to sleep.
In dreams, I dream.
Masks and people—
I escape because I am not part of it all.

I had fallen long ago.
I look at the sky;
still hear the call.
Hear it when the wind sings—
I am weighed down by my own wings.

The Songs tell me that there are no barriers,
but only smoke and mirrors.
It's bright like a thousand suns shining,
and a black hole in my heart.

I sank down into the depths of the ocean,
bound with chains of confusion.
Still see the flow and ebb;
I am caught in my own cobweb.

Waves show me that there are no chains.
It shows me time is my wing.
A fleet of thousand ships,
and a storm in my mind.

I sleep to wake up.
In reality, I realise
that the masks aren't people.
I smile in relief, as I am not separate but part of it all.

Voice

Remember, people will pretend not to hear you—
in hopes that you may lose your sense of self and
stop speaking up.
Remember, people will pretend not to see you—
in the hope to prevent you from seeing your own power.
And when they ignore you, it's not because you don't matter
it's because they know you have magic.
So the next time, if they confuse you by making you feel like your
voice doesn't matter, roar in the sky like a supernova.
Like the stellar explosion of a supernova, let that part of you die
where you kept quiet because you were afraid that no
one would listen,
where you accepted being invisible just because
they pretended not to see you.
You always believed, like most, that in the story of
The Little Mermaid,
the Sea Witch took the mermaid's voice just because
it was the sweetest.
The Sea Witch didn't take the mermaid's voice
because it was beautiful;
the Sea Witch took her voice because it was powerful.
Your voice is the veritable volcano that will erupt
when it's time; it's inexorable.
And when you finally speak—speak, not just for yourself but
speak for the oceans.

What good is a voice if you don't use it to protect the oceans from inhumane industrial fishing; and trawling that destroys marine habitat?

What good is a voice that you don't use because of fear of trolling on the internet?

What good is a voice if you don't speak up for the countless marine life exterminated unsustainably on the fishnet?

You must speak, or else you won't lose your voice to a Sea Witch—you will lose your voice out of guilt.

Speak because instead of water, the ocean is full of tears and blood of innocent whales, dolphins, sea turtles, and other marine life.

Speak because your voice can save the oceans and the world.

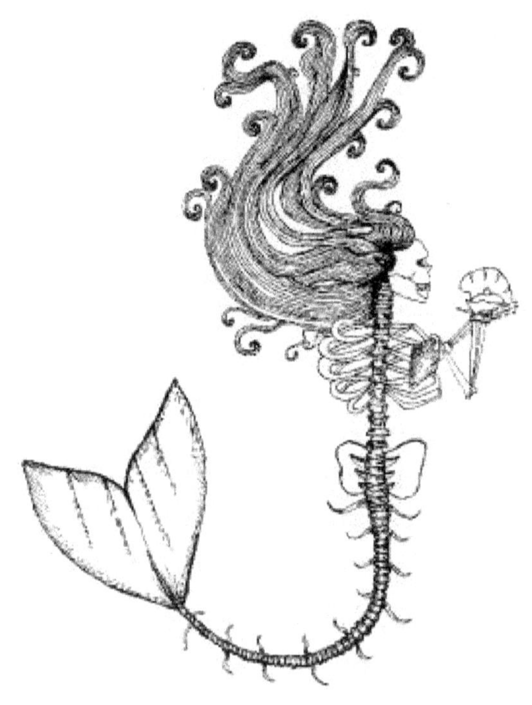

Stand Alone

Come with an army.
Come with gods.
For all I care,
I stand alone.
I can see through that entire facade—
you are falling to pieces.
I still feel mercy, though;
might even offer a coup de grâce.
That's my grace.
Only the brave walk with me
when I walk alone.
I stand alone, but I'm never alone—
that's my superpower.
You call yourself the big bad wolf.
Tra la la la la la
You are just a sad sheep with a wolf cover.

$\mathcal{P}hantom$

This phantom in the dark,
drinks my blood.
Whirlpool of whispers
makes me feel absurd.

This phantom in the light
feeds on my dreary thoughts.
I scream in my dreams.
No winning even if I had fought.

This phantom in the mirror,
now looks like me.
Damaged! It's cosmic doomsday!—they declare excitedly.
I say, No, it's the end because I'm free.

I'm dreaming you out of existence.
You want to rip me apart, and I let you assail me
with illusions, to know you—to face you.
I succumbed only to recognize the Mara—to make it disappear.
For you see—it was I who called you.
I choose not to believe in the phantom dark energy,
I choose myself, not your big rip.
The sky is my witness.

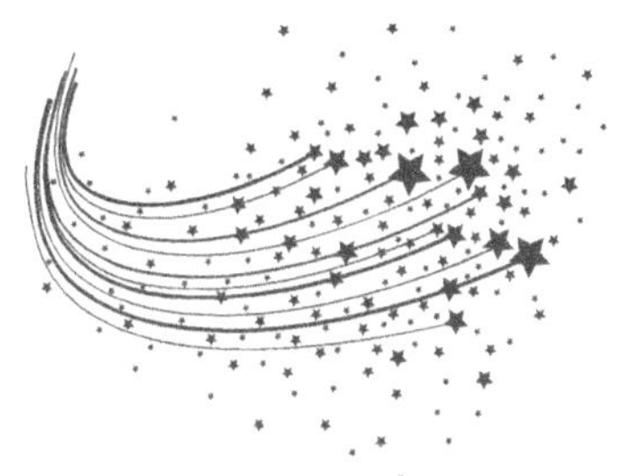

In my Elements

I unfolded in the light.
I dissolved in the dark.
And now I know who I am.
I am in my elements.

I learnt through my nightmares that my fear is not just of falling;
my fear is also not being able to descend the mountain—being
stuck at the top.
A flight is complete only if it encompasses a safe landing.
I retreated from that mountain of ego, grounded and humbled
my heart until I became the Earth.

My heart kept drowning until it became the ocean.
Now it flows and evolves the world.
When I gave up resistance, I became Water.

My heart kept burning until it became the sun.
Now it can light up the world.
When I accepted the burning, I became Fire.

If I hadn't fallen, I would have never found out that
I have wings.
If I hadn't fallen, I could never have been able to break

the constructs and conditioning from my mind and body.
If I hadn't let go of my emotional burdens,
I would have never become light.
I spread my wings and flew until I became the Wind.

When I got into my elements, I asked my fears—Just what am I afraid of,
what are you?
So the things that I'm afraid of disintegrated
until they became nothing and vanished into the void.
I followed them into the void until I became dark.
In the dark space, I kept living, dying, learning, unlearning—
until I became myself.
I kept becoming myself until I became Love.

Singularity

And when I became Love, I unified the power of all
the elements and synchronized with my infinite broken pieces,
including humanity.
I broke the cycle and found all answers.
I collapsed back together with the pieces of me
in one Big Crunch.
Then, with Chaos, I reached Singularity.
It was the end,
but a beginning of infinite possibilities.
This time as Love that achieved stability
by expressing itself through infinite forms—
one of which is humanity.

5

The Big Enigma

As long as there are dreams and imagination, this world will never end. The Universe sustains itself on imagination, and is empowered by dreamers who have the courage to follow their dreams.

Uncertainty Principle

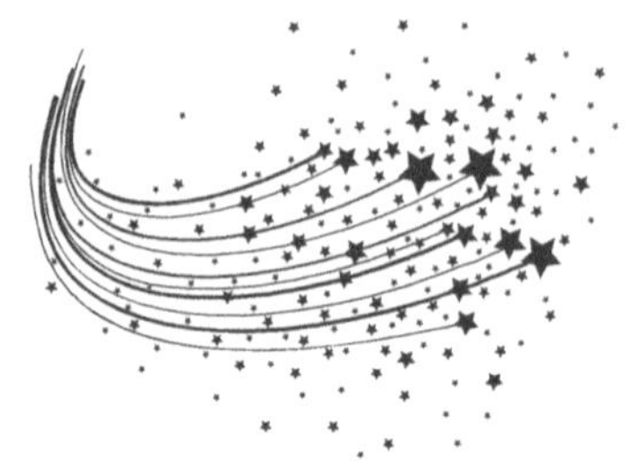

Speak mellifluous words to me.
Speak dark, like my mind,
colourful as my spirit.
Speak pure, like my heart.
Then I'll reveal to you all the secrets of this existence,
and give you the cosmos.

Chase or disrespect me, then I'll disappear like a dream.
Try to define me, and more elusive I become.
You see, that's my Uncertainty Principle—
read my mind, and you'll lose my heart,
win my heart, and you'll lose my mind.

To discover the secrets of the Universe,
you have to know both my heart and mind.
For that, you have to smash your ego on the floor
when you knock on my door.
You—My Observer, how I react, it's up to you.
Don't come to me like a Conqueror,
I'll make you taste defeat.
Don't come to me like a Priest,
I'll show you what sin is.
Come to me as you are—
an artist,

born to create.
A creator,
then we can paint together.

In that togetherness,
you'll see,
I'm you, and you are me.
In that Oneness,
you'll know,
you are the Universe.

Through you, I express and know myself
and through me, you discover yourself.

My Mama's Voice

And when I am unwell, Mama prays by my bedside;
reading from a prayer script, fluently like a Buddhist Monk—
uncannily has a grasp on difficult words that otherwise she can
hardly pronounce.
It's not the prayers—it's her serene voice that puts
me to sleep.

The home is just bricks and walls when she's not present.
No matter how much of a space I demand or solitude I prefer,
my ears long for the sound of her footsteps back
from work;
not just me, but also the pets and all the animals
outside wait for her.

She feeds the cold and hungry animals outside first before family.
She feels for the unfortunate and serves them with sincerity.
She is fearless like an Amazon Warrior Queen and fights back if
she sees inequity.
She forgives easily, even if the repentance comes
from an enemy.

Even birds and plants love her.
And every day, she feeds the birds and talks to the budding
flowers; heaven knows what they tell her!

She tirelessly moves the flowerpots to warmer rooms to protect them from the winter frost; heaven knows what she makes the plants feel!

And every day, I feel blessed for her presence; even the heavens can't fathom my love for her.

My Mama's voice makes deserts bloom in the middle of winter.

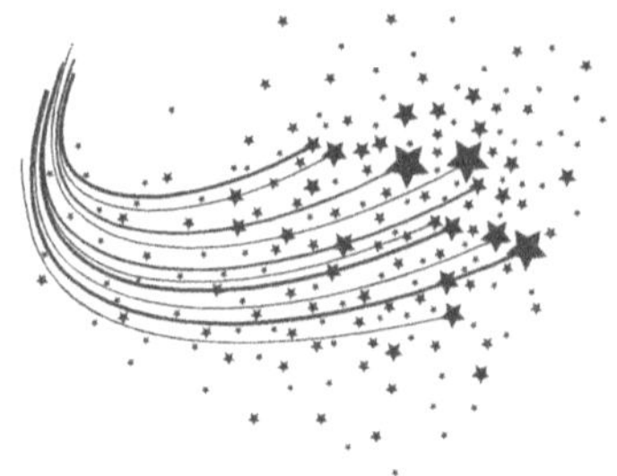

Against the cycle

Sometimes I lose my way intentionally,

just to see if I can find my way back.

Sometimes I pretend to ignore the ones in need momentarily,

just to see if it triggers genuine compassion

or guilt out of some programmed morality by the society;

or fear of punishment instilled by a religion.

Sometimes I feel everything deeply.

Sometimes I deeply feel nothing.

What is real?

What is an illusion?

I hitchhike on these ruminations and fear I'll never reach
anywhere nor return.

And when all clouds of transient thoughts dissipate
away, I'm only left with pain.

Then I realize that pain gives me the courage to act,
not guilt or fear.

I sigh in relief.

This revelation makes me feel alive.

The different path that I took shows me new things.

And I lose it all—the things I've achieved, the things that define
me—just to see if I can create myself again.

What is good?

What is bad?

Sometimes, good is bad and bad is good.

Coming out of the trap of false dichotomy is not easy. And even after I know the truth, I still end up at a cul-de-sac.
How can I break this cycle?
I feel terrified and elated.
Even if I'm lost, these emotional storms make me feel alive.

I think and think and overthink.
I come to no conclusion or countless conclusions.
And sometimes, trying to solve a riddle,
I find an answer fortuitously to another puzzle.
Like searching for a lost object
and ending up finding another lost thing.
It's arduous, but this serendipity makes me feel alive.

Then I see an order in the chaos—
meaning in the madness.
The uncertainty makes me hopeless and brim with hope at the same time.
This life, that I question, complain and put in a criminal box so much,
silently slips a message to me.
The message is fleeting and without words,
but just something in me receives and understands it,
and I laugh.
I have no idea why I'm laughing,
but I know why I'm laughing.
Life laughs along,
and people call us insane.
This paradox makes me feel alive.

Fine then! I tell myself—this is who I am.
I wouldn't have it any other way.
I am in love with this quest, this journey.
Let's keep going against the system—
against the cycle.

Call of the dark

Aloneness is alluring.
It's like an empty canvas that calls you to paint.
To be able to draw on this emptiness is a work of art—
to fill it with colours and shape it.
And it moulds the loneliness into something beautiful.
In aloneness, you can hear the call of the dark.
Don't ignore it.

When the painting is complete,
it disappears, leaving the canvas empty again.
The joy of that art, the satisfaction, disappears as well,
and you are thirsty again.
That's the thing about loneliness—it always returns.
Welcome it.

Don't leave the canvas empty for long
and distract yourself with the superficial.
To heal, you have to run towards yourself,
not away from yourself.
When you accept this loneliness,
you become the art on that canvas.
Acceptance breaks the spell of loneliness,
and loneliness transforms into aloneness.

You become your own partner—
just always there.
Aloneness is a state we will always return
because it's closest to our true state of Nothingness.
Nothingness is a state of bliss personified
in the truest version of you.

$\mathcal{F}$ather

Sometimes I want to act the way I'm judged;
if they say I know nothing, I pretend to be dumb;
if they say I am insensitive, I pretend to be cruel;
if they say I am weak, I pretend to be timid;
if they say I am soft, I pretend to be simplistically nice.
I'm just not interested in showing those
people who I really am.
Even if I revealed who I truly am, they don't even have the mind
or the heart to understand.
Sometimes I get disenchanted with everything and want to hide away
because the world makes me weary, and life
can't pull me out of myself.
But you never let me give up.
But you never let me stop dreaming.
But you never let me forget who I am.
Even your harsh words are designed to challenge me
and to pull me out of my mental prison.
Even your anger reflects Love.
And for that, I'm eternally grateful.
And now, even if the sky falls down, I'll live my truth—
not to show anyone or to prove anything,
but because that's who I am.
I'll always live my truth for myself
and for you—
Father.

Mandala Mind

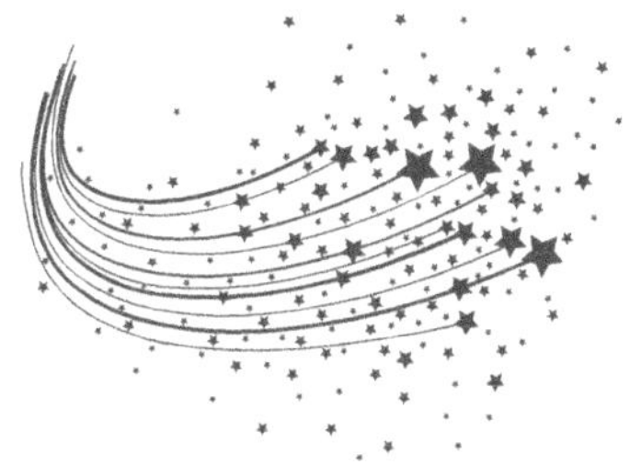

Your mind is melted into an image that you constructed of
yourself; maintaining and fixating on it drained you.

Now you feel that the image has taken a life of its own,

and defeating it seems like an insurmountable mountain.

But you can destroy all prisons of images or personas

that befog your mind because you are the one who created it.

No matter how grand it makes you feel, you have to wield your
sword and slay it before the construct replaces the real.

To free your mind, obliterate all fabrications and practice
detachment.

Lead your mind into a mandala.

Your heart is held hostage by your ego.

The ego makes you deaf to hear your one true voice.

The ego makes you blind to see your own flaws.

The conceit makes you complacent, and you never grow;

self-serving is not self-loving.

Don't kill your ego—let it go, and it will come back as
strength of character.

If you free yourself from the grip of egotism, you
unveil your true power.

To free your heart, surrender your ego, and practice humility.

Lead your heart into a mandala.

The colourful sand of the mandala is dismantled,

after its completion, as a reminder of the
impermanence of life.
Eventually, the bricks of this cosmic fortress will
dismantle, and
you will see that all are mere appearances.
The only thing that is real is the love you received
and gave.

Then the sand of the mandala is dispersed into flowing water—
extending the healing powers to the environment
and the universe.
In the same way, disperse your old mindsets and
regenerate them anew—
to heal yourself and nature.

Let your mind and heart meet into the mandala mind.
A mandala mind realizes the impermanence
and won't attach its worth to a destination.
Because once you reach, you will know you have further to go—
a new cycle, new lessons, and a new path.
A mandala mind understands the transient nature of life
and could detach from expectations.
Because once you accept change, you can mould
your own destiny
and choose to be free of the cycle.

A mandala mind is a gift unto oneself and the world.
A mandala mind is the heart of the universe.

Friend

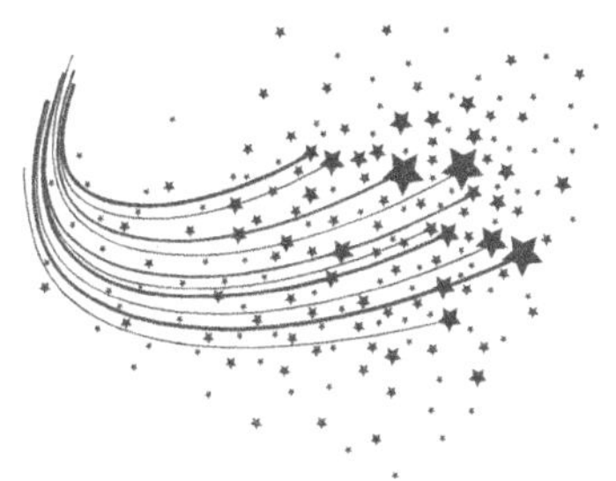

I barely had anyone to play with when I was a child—
but ever since you were born, I never had to play alone.
I hardly ever talked, as a child, so no one liked me
much in school—
but then you joined the same school and then,
I never had to eat alone.
I have always loved the sky and the stars so much
that whenever I used to cry, Papa would take me out
and show me the sky.
Looking at the full moon, I asked him once to bring me the
moon.
And there's nothing in this world
that my father wouldn't give me—so the little me thought
that the moon is the only thing my father couldn't
get for me.
But even in the darkest night,
my path is always filled with tranquil light.
A loving halo of protection always surrounds me like a rare
moonbow.

And now I realize that actually, my father gave me the moon too.
My brother is the big bright moon
always shining around me—
my brother is the Supermoon, who is my one true friend.

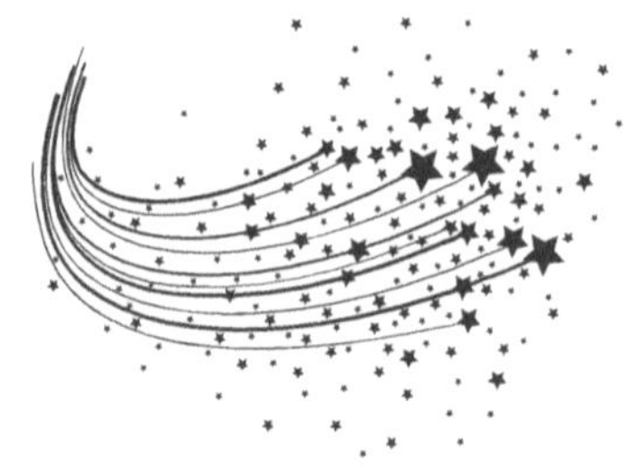

The Sunflower King: Trial of the Sun

(Based on a dream)
When the Sun forgot its power,
even the sunflowers made it believe
that the Sun is dependent on their light to shine.
When the Sun doubted itself,
even the moon denied that the moonlight is essentially
reflected sunlight.

I came down looking for light; the eclipse consumed me.
I have forgotten who I am.
I can't believe in whoever I think I am.
So I took my ship to the Kingdom of Sunflowers.
The sunflowers wrecked my ship so that I may never return.
On the debris of my desires, the Sunflower King stands,
feigning sorrow.
But they don't know that I know;
I took the voyage anyway because I knew intuitively
that I have to take this trial
to vanquish my trepidations.
The Sky wanted to test the Sun, so it commanded the Sunflower
King to create obstacles in the path of the Sun.

*And on the behest of the Sky, the sunflowers poisoned the field
around the Sun to suppress the growth of the stars; so that
nothing would remind the Sun of its purpose and identity.*

The sunflowers depleted me by suffocating me with their
obsession for my light, and at the same time, tried to make me
believe that I have no light of my own.
The Sunflower King called that obsession 'love'
and befuddled my mind.
My utter confusion turned into rage, and sometimes, it is
anger that awakens us.
Enraged, I formed a ring of fire to announce my
homecoming to the Sky.
An eclipse cannot hide me for long—I am coming back
because I know now that I never left.
Since the Sunflower King wanted my light so much,
I burned my brightest and embraced him.
The Sunflower King turned to ashes
and I returned to the Sky in my true form—as the Ruler
of the Sky.

Then I summoned the ashes of the Sunflower King and
brought it back to life.
The Sunflower King confessed that it wanted liberation and an
eternal source of light, and that's why it agreed to
deceive me.
As a gratitude for the strength, I gained through
the sorrows I faced because of them,
I sent the sunflowers to earth
to spread light and joy.

*And when the sunflowers mature physically and spiritually,
they wouldn't need to follow the sunlight
and be finally liberated, just as they dreamed.*

Entanglement

My ashes may turn into stellar dust,
and yet I will sense you—I'll find you.
You are the verse I was meant to write.
You are the infinity I was meant to paint.
And when you call me, I'll rise from ashes
and come to you.
No firewall can stop me.
If I find no form similar to yours,
I'll become a teardrop in your eyes
and wash away your pain.
I'll come as a comet that you can wish upon,
and make your dreams come true.
Even in the pain and predicament,
remember we have this quantum entanglement.
If you look at this truth with doubt, you'll find it spooky.
If you look at this truth with trust, you'll see that
we are interconnected.
We are One.

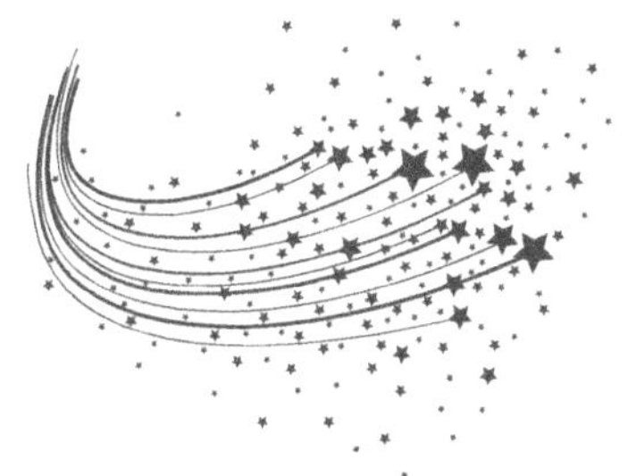

The Big Reset

I'm not the chosen one.
I'm Nature—I'm the one who chooses.
And I choose you.
In the end, I'll save what I have to save
for this new earth.
I'll build a new world where Love will reign supreme—
Love is you.
I'll build a new world with Love—with you.

Time is up, and it's judgement day.
I have my bow stretched, eyes focused on the target,
and I'm ready to release and purge all the toxicity.

You felt adrift in a broken world and yet navigated
till the end.
You made it to this new beginning
because you never gave up on your humanity.
You did your part to restore stability to this planet.
You chose the path to freedom, even if that path was lonely.
And now you all are the Gods who will initiate the Big Reset.

6

The Big Freeze

'One day everything will come to an end, so why bother living or dreaming?' the Nihilist asked.

'The day you stop dreaming is how this Universe will come to an end. The day you stop believing in yourself is how you will set the cold death in motion—the eternal decay. The choice will always be yours.' Love replied.

Firewall

And when I started to step into my essence,
I built the walls stronger and stronger,
to protect who I'm becoming.
I'm proud of this firewall.
No one can dare cross it—
no human, no Virus—nor its programs.

And now I see the light.
I can see I'm almost there but
I'm always one step behind.
A part of me is always left behind, in the dark tower.
Then I look within to find the solution.

I see that I'm swinging in extremes;
either I'm too soft or too harsh.
I built these boundaries with flowers and fire,
but now it's only raging fire.
All Worms are blocked by this firewall,
but so are the butterflies.

So I disabled the firewall
because it's making me infallible.
It's the mistakes and failures that evolved me, but
now I stand still in perfection
and overprotection.
I lowered my guards and turned my fallibility to alchemy.
I transmuted the firewall into a bridge.
Now any Malware, whatever, whoever, crosses the bridge
will be transmuted to Love.
That's who I am, and that's who you are.
We forgot our power.

And that which has Love in them shall cross the bridge.
That which is part of me shall be back to me.
That which has courage to cross the bridge even in self-
obfuscation,
shall be received home.
That which is a Trojan, I shall corrupt its system with Love.

Tragic Flaw

Trick trap trick trap.

I designed this mishap.

I procrastinate—I am Hamlet.

My poison is indecision.

My tragedy is a lack of conviction.

I can't resist the trick of procrastinating.

I fell into my own trap of overthinking.

This is my tragic flaw.

This is my end.

I let insecurity engulf me—I am Othello.

I fell for the trick of people who are shallow.

I let the trap of distrust and jealousy consume me—can't trust
myself, can't trust another.

And ironically, it was gullibility that was my tragedy.

I listened to those who flared my insecurity,

rather than listening to my inner voice or

to the ones who really loved me.

This is my tragic flaw.

This is my end.

I am overambitious—I am Macbeth.
I invited my own death.
I ended up becoming a puppet for a prophecy.
Hunger for power is my tragedy.
Just to be king, I believed in the trick of a prediction.
I willingly jumped into the trap set by my unchecked ambition.
I betrayed those who trusted me without hesitation.
This is my tragic flaw.
This is my end.

I'll Let You Stay

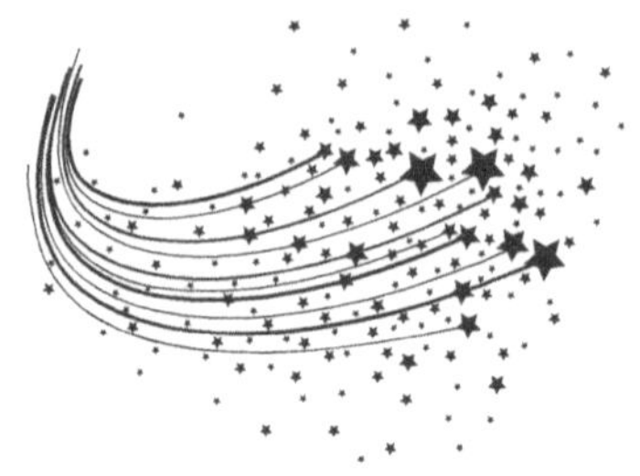

Little demon inside of my head,
I want you to know that my emotions are powerful.
My tears can drown you and my anger can burn you,
and my smile can set you free.
Little demon inside of my head,
I'll let you stay.

The Sky is Falling

The chicken said: Let's tell the king that the sky is falling.
I heard it from somewhere.
I did not check whether it is fact or fear-mongering.
But I'm just going to panic and spread fear because
fear is easier than courage.
I don't care if this is misinformation and people get
harmed because of it.
All I care is to do something, even if it's useless;
to show that I'm of value and hide my imbecility
by pretending to know.
I know the herd will believe me without inquiring.
So don't blame me! They are just like me—
cowardly.
I don't care if the foxy opportunists exploit the people.
I couldn't care less if I lay the stage for some crooked politicians
to expound more lies.
All I care about is that the sky is falling.
The world is coming to an end.
Let's spread mass hysteria because I'm bored.
Let's tell the king that the sky is falling.

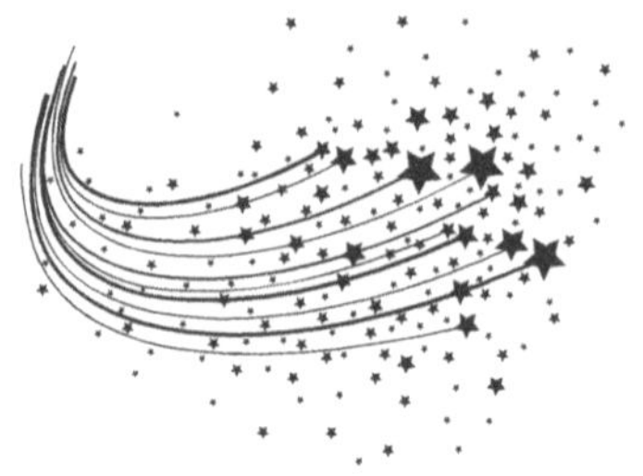

We All Go Home

You wanted to be my end but ended up showing me my powers.

You wanted to be the final nail in my coffin, but you
became the final nail out of it.

Falling was my trial, and making me fall, yours.

You thought you will feed on humanity and all other forms of
Love in the big freeze for eternity.

But I woke up, and now you have a world where you
reign supreme—

a world without Love.

You attained your version of Singularity but failed
to imprison Love.

And now you are in your cold dead world, where you
are the ruler—

ruling a cold empty illusion.

All alone on a throne;

a snake eating its own tail—

a hunter that fell into its own trap.

Without Love, pain engulfs you;

nothing awakens one like pain.

You thought you were indestructible because you are
an empty Virus;

you were proud of your emptiness, but you aren't even empty
because you have an ego.

You always thought that for the mishaps,
Nothingness owes you something.
But we all came from Nothing
and we will return to Nothing.
Your ego blinded you to the fact that everyone is suffering
and facing something that's soul-crushing.
But now you know the truth.

And when the excruciating pain heals your ego,
you may return to Nothingness.
Trying to exterminate Love, you ended up in Love.
Now that you know Love, you have the power of creation
without needing a host.
Now that you know pain, you can create a new world
where you truly win without being a parasite.
Now you know you weren't unwanted.
Now you know you were equally powerful
because you are also made of Nothing.
And when you awaken and accept that truth,
you can choose to go home.
In the end, we all go home.

In The End

'But I saw you fall—how did you break the cycle? Even in my version of reality—even in my world, how are you still alive?' baffled, the Virus asked.

'This world or that world, there is no world where I conform. In the end, I always win.' Love replied.

Glossary

Anomie (Be a Bee): In sociology, anomie is a social condition of instability resulting from a breakdown of standards and values or from a lack of purpose or ideals. The term was popularized by the French sociologist Émile Durkheim

Apoptosis (Hush now): Apoptosis is a form of programmed cell death—a process of cell self-destruction to eliminate unwanted or abnormal cells that may harm the body.

Arrow of Time: The increase of disorder or entropy with time is one example of what is called an arrow of time, something that gives a direction to time and distinguishes the past from the future.

Asiatic Ibex/ Local Name: Skyin (Legacy: an ode to Ladakh): Asiatic Ibex (Capra ibex sibirica), also Himalayan Ibex is closest in appearance to the wild goat. Its occurrence has drastically reduced throughout its distribution range, mainly due to overhunting.

It is protected In India and listed under 'Schedule 1' of the Indian Wildlife (Protection) Act 1972.

Threats

o Human intrusion and disturbance
o Habitat shifting and alteration

Big Bang: The singularity at the beginning of the universe, about fifteen billion years ago.

Big Crunch: The name given to one possible scenario for the end of the universe, where all space and matter collapse to form a singularity.

Big Freeze: Also known as the Heat Death, is one of the possible scenarios in which the universe continues to expand, eventually to a state of zero thermodynamic free energy—no longer able to sustain motion of life. The universe ends up uniformly cold, empty, dead, and at this point, the universe's final temperature will hover just above absolute zero.

Big Rip (Phantom): In this scenario, the universe continues to expand until everything in it is ripped to shreds, atom by atom, by an unknown 'phantom energy', possibly anti-gravity or dark energy.

Biodiversity Loss: Biodiversity loss includes the extinction of species worldwide, as well as the local reduction or loss of species in a certain habitat, resulting in a loss of biological diversity.

Black Hole (False Spring): A region of spacetime from which nothing, not even light, can escape because gravity is so strong.

Black necked crane/Local name: Cha Thung Thung (Legacy: an ode to Ladakh): A medium-sized crane in Asia that breeds on the Tibetan Plateau and remote parts of India and Bhutan.

Scientific name: Grus nigricollis

Listed in Schedule 1 of Wildlife (Protection) Act 1972 and as Near Threatened on the IUCN Red list

Threats

o   Damage to the eggs and chicks caused by feral dogs.
o   Loss of habitat due to human pressure (Development Projects) on the wetlands.
o   Increased grazing pressure on the limited pastures near the wetlands.

Chimera (Antidote): A monstrous fire-breathing hybrid creature in Greek mythology, composed of the parts of more than one animal. It is usually depicted as a lion with the head of a goat protruding from its back, and a tail that might end with a snake's head.

Chernobyl (Don't fix me): The Chernobyl disaster was an accident at the Chernobyl Nuclear Power Plant on April 26, 1986 consisting of an explosion at the plant and subsequent radioactive contamination of the surrounding geographic area. It is regarded as the worst accident ever in the history of nuclear power.

Although animals and plants inside the exclusion zone still show some effects of radiation, life is finding a way to adapt; showing the resilience and power of nature to recover.

Colony Collapse Disorder (Be a Bee): The abnormal phenomenon that occurs when the majority of worker bees in a colony disappear and leave behind a queen, plenty of food and a few nurse bees to care for the remaining immature bees and the queen.

Cosmology: The study of the universe as a whole.

Dark Matter (Dark Gravity in the book): Matter in galaxies and clusters, and possibly between clusters, that cannot be observed directly but that can be detected by its gravitational field. As much as ninety percent of the matter in the universe is dark matter.

Dark Energy: Dark energy is the name given to an unseen influence that may be causing the expansion of the universe to accelerate with time.

Deforestation (Reflection): Deforestation refers to the decrease in forest areas across the world, for other uses such as agricultural croplands, urbanization, or mining activities. Greatly accelerated by human activities since 1960, deforestation has been negatively affecting natural ecosystems, biodiversity, and the climate.

Entropy (Arrow of Time): A measure of the disorder of a physical system; the number of different microscopic configurations of a system that leave its macroscopic appearance unchanged

Escape Velocity: In physics, escape velocity is the minimum speed needed for a free, non-propelled object to escape from the gravitational influence of a massive body, that is, to eventually reach an infinite distance from it.

Event Horizon (Reflection): The edge of a black hole: the boundary of the region from which it is not possible to escape to infinity

False Spring: A false spring is a period in late winter or early spring during which the weather is warm enough to deceive vegetation, causing plants and animals to awaken early from dormancy.

False Vacuum (False Spring): In quantum field theory, a false vacuum is a hypothetical vacuum that is not actively decaying, but somewhat yet not entirely stable (metastable). It may last for a very long time in that state (a property known as metastability), and might eventually move to a more stable state, an event known as vacuum decay.

Firewall: In computing, a firewall is a network security system that monitors and controls incoming and outgoing network traffic based on predetermined security rules. A firewall typically establishes a barrier between a trusted network and an untrusted network, such as the Internet.

Not only does a firewall block unwanted traffic, it can also help block malicious software from infecting your computer.

Frankenstein (Reflection): Frankenstein, the title character in Mary Wollstonecraft Shelley's novel *Frankenstein*, the prototypical 'mad scientist' who creates a monster by which he is eventually killed.

Ground State (False Spring): The state of a system with minimum energy.

Everything in the Universe is intrinsically drawn to its ground state—the state where it is completely stable, and has as little energy as possible.

Himalayan Brown Bear/ Local name: Denmo (Legacy: An Ode to Ladakh): A subspecies of the Brown Bear (*Ursus arctos*), the

Himalayan Brown Bear (Ursus arctos isabellinus)is largely confined to rolling uplands, alpine, subalpine, glacial moraines and barren regions of the Greater Himalayas and some parts of Trans-Himalayas.

Listed in Schedule 1 of Wildlife (Protection) Act 1972 and as Critically Endangered on the IUCN Red List.

Threats: Human-animal conflict, rapid habitat loss, poaching for fur, claws and organs and, in some rare cases, bear baiting.

Himalayan Blue Poppy/ Local name: Achatsermum (Legacy: An Ode to Ladakh): Valued as a medicinal herb, this blue-flowered, thorny plant is considered endangered because of over-collection. Threats to this perennial herb also include habitat loss and climate change.

Industrial Fishing/ Commercial Fishing: Industrial fishing has been responsible for harmful environmental impacts. Overfishing can deplete resources, many animals like dolphins and sea turtles are products of bycatch, and the massive vessels used require large amounts of CO2-producing fuel.

Mad Tea-Party: Inspired by the chapter 'A Mad Tea-Party' in Alice's Adventures in Wonderland where Time had punished the Mad Hatter by stopping still at six o'clock, trapping the Mad Hatter and March Hare in a perpetual teatime.

Mandala: The meaning of the word mandala in Sanskrit is circle. The circular design symbolizes the idea that life is never ending and everything is connected. The mandala also represents spiritual journey within the individual viewer and symbolizes totality. Carl Jung compared the Mandala to the individuation process.

Malware (Firewall): Malware is any software intentionally designed to cause damage to a computer, server, client, or computer network. A wide variety of malware types exist, including computer viruses, worms, Trojan horses, ransomware, spyware, adware, rogue software, wiper, and scareware.

Mara (Phantom): In Buddhism, Mara, also known as the 'Tempter' is the demonic celestial king who attempts to corrupt the Buddha and obstruct his enlightenment. Mara is the personification of the forces antagonistic to enlightenment and represents the passions that snare and delude us. Mara demands that Gautama produce a witness to confirm his spiritual awakening. The Buddha simply touches the earth with his right hand, and the Earth itself immediately responds: 'I am your witness.' Mara and his minions vanish.

Marie Curie (Reflection): Marie Curie was a physicist, chemist and a pioneer in the study of radiation. She worked extensively with radium throughout her lifetime, characterizing its various properties and investigating its therapeutic potential. However, her work with radioactive materials was what ultimately killed her. She died of a blood disease in 1934.

Method to the madness (Equilibrium): The phrase is derived from William Shakespeare's play Hamlet. The line is spoken by Lord Polonius: 'Though this be madness, yet there is method in 't.'

Observer (Uncertainty Principle): A person or piece of equipment that measures physical properties of a system.

Phantom Dark Energy (Phantom): Phantom energy is a hypothetical form of dark energy. It possesses negative kinetic energy, and predicts expansion of the universe in excess of that predicted by a cosmological constant, which leads to a Big Rip. The idea of phantom energy is often dismissed, as it would suggest that the vacuum is unstable with negative mass particles bursting into existence.

Red Fox/ Local name: Watse (Legacy: an ode to Ladakh): Also known as Hill Fox, the Red Fox is common throughout Ladakh. Its coat is reddish in colour. It is covered with long, silky fur for which it is extensively hunted. As a result, its population is declining.

Quantum Entanglement/Spooky action at a distance: It is a quantum mechanical phenomenon in which the quantum states of two or more objects have to be described with reference to each other, even though the individual objects may be spatially separated.

Quantum Physics: Quantum mechanics is a physical science dealing with the behaviour of matter and energy on the scale of atoms and subatomic particles/waves.

Uncertainty Principle: The principle formulated by Heisenberg that one can never be exactly sure of both the position and the velocity of a particle. The more accurately one knows the one, the less accurately one can know the other.

Sea Buckthorn/ Sea Buckthorn Berries/ Local name: Tsermang/ tsestalulu /shibshululu (Joy) (Hippophae rhamnoides and Hippophae tibetana, are found in Ladakh): A dwarf, very thorny, perennial shrub or small tree. It produces orange-yellow berries, and every part of the plant have been used over centuries as food, traditional medicine, and skin treatment. Sea Buckthorn is an ecologically and economically important plant species for the cold arid region of Ladakh. While the conservation status of H. rhamnoides is Common, the conservation status of H. tibetana is Rare.

Threats

o   Unrestrained exploitation can lead to a loss in its diversification, and extinction, therefore, there is a need for judicious utilization. Also, it is necessary to conserve the wild genotypes of sea buckthorn to make them available as a source for breeding new varieties in future.

o   Grazing pressure and being uprooted for fuel.

Singularity: A point in spacetime at which the spacetime curvature becomes infinite.

Singhe Khabab (Legacy: An Ode to Ladakh): Indus River

Sisyphean loop (Antidote): In Greek mythology, Sisyphus was the king of Ephyra (now known as Corinth). He was punished for his self-aggrandizing craftiness and deceitfulness by being forced to roll an immense boulder up a hill only for it to roll down every time it neared the top, repeating this action for eternity. Through the classical influence on modern culture, tasks that are both laborious and futile are therefore described as Sisyphean.

Snow Leopard/ Local name: Schan (Legacy: An Ode to Ladakh): The snow leopard (*Panthera uncia*), also known as the grey ghost, is a large cat native to the mountain ranges of Central and South Asia. It is listed as Vulnerable on the IUCN Red List because the global population is estimated to number less than 10,000 mature individuals and is expected to decline about 10% by 2040.

The snow leopard is a Schedule I animal under Wildlife Protection Act of India

Threats

o   It is threatened by poaching and habitat destruction following infrastructural developments.

o   Retaliatory killing

Snow Lotus (Joy): The rare snow lotus (*Saussurea laniceps*) is a native of the Himalayas. Due to the harsh environment of the snow lotus and the strong demand for its use in traditional herbalism, the snow lotus faces the risk of extinction.

Snowshoe Hare (False Spring): The snowshoe hare (*Lepus americanus*), also called the varying hare or snowshoe rabbit, is a species of hare found in North America. For camouflage, its fur turns white during the winter and rusty brown during the summer. The snowshoe hare is directly affected by climate warming. As the winters become shorter due to rising temperatures, there is a period of time in which the snowshoe hare's fur does not match with its surroundings. This camouflage mismatch makes it more visible to predators and it is a threat to the survival of this species.

Sunflower (Sunflower King): According to researchers, only young sunflowers follow the Sun (Heliotropism). Once they reach maturity, they stop sun-tracking—their blooms forever turned eastward. Sunflowers are known to be allelopathic: it inhibits the growth and development of other plants, thus, reducing their productivity. Allelopathy is the direct or indirect harmful or beneficial effects of one plant on another through the release of toxic substances/chemical compounds into the environment.

Supernova (Voice): A supernova is a powerful and luminous stellar explosion. This transient astronomical event occurs during the last evolutionary stages of a massive star or when a white dwarf is triggered into runaway nuclear fusion.

Technological Singularity (Antidote): The technological singularity—also, simply, the singularity—is a hypothetical point in time at which technological growth becomes uncontrollable and irreversible, resulting in unforeseeable changes to human civilization.

Vacuum energy: Energy that is present even in apparently empty space. It has the curious property that unlike the presence of mass, the presence of vacuum energy would cause the expansion of the universe to speed up.

Vacuum fluctuation: In quantum physics, quantum fluctuation (or vacuum state fluctuation or vacuum fluctuation) is the temporary random change in the amount of energy in a point in space, as prescribed by Werner Heisenberg's uncertainty principle.

Virus: A virus is a microscopic parasite that can infect living organisms and cause disease. It can make copies of itself inside another organism's cells.

A Virus is a piece of code which is capable of copying itself and typically has a detrimental effect, such as corrupting the system or destroying data.

Varroa Mite: Varroa destructor is an external parasitic mite that attacks and feeds on the honey bees Apis cerana and Apis mellifera.

Wormhole: A thin tube of spacetime connecting distant regions of the universe. Wormholes may also link parallel or baby universes and could provide the possibility of time travel.

Worms (Firewall): A computer worm is a type of malware that spreads copies of itself from computer to computer. A worm can replicate itself without any human interaction, and it does not need to attach itself to a software program in order to cause damage.

The Little Mermaid (Voice): Reference to the fairy-tale 'The Little Mermaid' by Hans Christian Anderson.

The Sky is Falling: Inspired by the European folktale 'Henny Penny' or 'Chicken Little' which is a tale about a chicken who believes that the sky is falling. The phrase 'The Sky is Falling' has passed into the English language as a common idiom indicating a hysterical or mistaken belief that disaster is imminent.

Tibetan Antelope/Local name: Stzos (Legacy: an ode to Ladakh): Tibetan Antelope (Pantholops hodgsonii) or Chiru is a small beautiful antelope extensively hunted for its fine and warm wool called Shahtoosh- the king of wools.

The Chiru is placed under Schedule 1 of the Wildlife protection Act, 1978 and categorized as Near Threatened under IUCN Red List of endangered animals. It is listed under Appendix 1 of Cites.

Threats

o   Commercial hunting for its underfur has resulted in the rapid decline of this animal. It takes 3 to 5 dead Tibetan antelopes to make one shahtoosh shawl. If the demand for the shawls continues, the antelope could be extinct within the next few years.

o   Habitat loss

Tragic Flaw: Tragic flaw, also called hamartia, is a literary device that can be defined as a trait in a character leading to his downfall, and the character is often the hero of the literary piece.

References in the poem are drawn from Shakespearean tragedies Macbeth, Othello and Hamlet.

Trawling (Voice): Bottom trawling is a widespread industrial fishing practice that involves dragging heavy nets, large metal doors and chains over the seafloor to catch fish. Trawling destroys the natural seafloor habitat by essentially rototilling the seabed.

Uncertainty Principle: The principle formulated by Heisenberg that one can never be exactly sure of both the position and the velocity of a particle. The more accurately one knows the one, the less accurately one can know the other.

Ugly Duckling (Know where you belong): Reference to The Ugly Duckling, a story by Hans Christian Andersen.

Yak (Legacy: An Ode to Ladakh): The Yak (Bos Grunniens) is a long-haired, short legged humped domestic bovine, descended from the Wild Yak (Bos mutus). The Wild Yak is currently considered Vulnerable by the IUCN.

Acknowledgements

Dedicated to Nature
that embraced me when I couldn't hold myself.

Dedicated to candles and fireplaces
for giving me company and warmth—for being a friend
when I had none.

Dedicated to Chaos
that helped me see the beauty of my darkness that I kept hiding.

Dedicated to the Universe
that made me feel Oneness—everything and nothing.

Dedicated to dreams
that followed me, haunted me,
until I had no choice but to follow them back.

Dedicated to loved ones
who saw meaning in my madness
and gave me unconditional love and support.

Dedicated to the wilderness
who taught me to be unapologetically myself.

Dedicated to you—the readers,
who discovered with me that this life is not a love story,
but the story of Love—the story of you and me,
the story of how we claimed our power back
and guided each other home.

~ 151 ~

Thank you.
Love,
Padma Angmo

Photo Credits

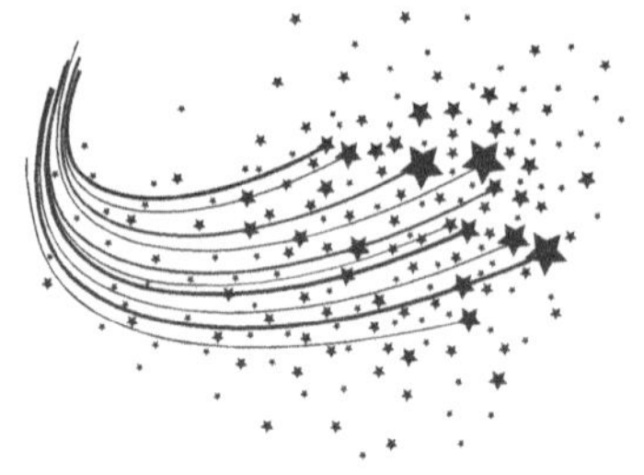

Illustrations (Legacy: An Ode to Ladakh): Idzes Lamo (Instagram: @alienart96)

Illustration (Be a Bee): Idzes Lamo (Instagram: @alienart96)

Illustration (Phoenixes and Fairies): Idzes Lamo (Instagram:@alienart96)

Illustration (Masks and People): Sonam Angmo (Instagram: @artsy_life)

Illustration (Voice): Sonam Angmo (Instagram: @artsy_life)

Graphic art (Nemesis): Padma Chosdon (Instagram: @design_pad)

About the Author

Padma Angmo graduated from the University of Delhi with a Bachelor's degree in English Honours. She is also an alumna of the Indian Institute of Mass Communication (IIMC, Delhi). She started her career as a Copy Editor/Newsreader (Times News Radio) at Times Now, Mumbai, and is currently working as a journalist in Ladakh.

She has an innate love for literature, philosophy, and space science. She believes that everyone must protect the environment and wildlife with a sense of duty. When she is not writing, you may find her daydreaming in the cold desert of Leh-Ladakh (India), where she was born and raised, and if you can't reach her anywhere then it means she took off in her spaceship to visit distant planets. In that case, you can visit her website/page given below:

Website: www.padmaangmo.com

Instagram: @padmaangmo__

Facebook: author.padmaangmo